GOD AND YOU: PERSON TO PERSON

Developing a Daily Personal Relationship with Jesus

by Anthony M. Coniaris

D1452963

LIGHT & LIFE PUBLIJHING
Minneapolis, Minnesota

Light and Life Publishing Company
P.O. Box 26421
Minneapolis, MN 55426-0421

ISBN 1-880971-11-9

Table of Contents

Chapter One

A Personal Sense of Involvement with God

Come, my Light, and illumine my darkness.
Come, my Life, and revive me from death.
Come, my Physician, and heal my wounds.
Come, Flame of divine love, and burn up the
   thorns of my misdeeds, kindling my heart
   with the flame of Your love.
Come, my God, sit upon the throne of my
   heart and reign there.
For You alone are my God and my Lord.

   – St. Dimitrii of Rostov, 17th Century

A PERSONAL SENSE OF INVOLVEMENT WITH GOD

A sociologist and priest, Thomas M. Gannon of Loyola University, tested out the platitude that if a boy went to church more often, he would not get into trouble. His findings were astounding. He tested 150 Roman Catholic teenaged boys at the Cook County juvenile detention center. Most of the boys in the study were, by any standard, religious: 53 percent attended mass once or twice a month, and another 27 percent attended mass every Sunday.

And they did more than simply turn up in church; they believed in God (only 19 percent denied His existence). Most of them said they prayed often, they were aware of the doctrines of the Catholic Church in regard to stealing, sex, and gang fighting, and most of them agreed that these doctrines were right.

Despite their evident religious commitment, however, the gap between what these boys did and what they said was enormous. Why?

This is the astounding discovery of this priest-sociologist. He discovered that in parochial schools and in sermons, these boys had been taught a creed, and intellectually they accepted that creed as true. What was entirely missing from their religious experience, however, was any personal sense of involvement with God. Not one thought that God took an interest in him individually. Many could not even think of themselves as worthy of God's interest or love.

The conclusion was that religious faith exerts its strongest influence when there is a personal, felt relationship between the individual and God. If this is lacking, then religious faith is no match for the adolescent gang.

Many young people and adults have never had a clear personal encounter with the person of Jesus. All they've experienced in their church is a discipline or an institution. They learn the commandments, but not the loving God behind the commandments. What they need most is a revelation of Jesus Christ as a loving, compassionate God, Who is vitally and personally interested in each one of them; like the God of St. Paul who described Jesus as the One "Who loved me and gave Himself for me." Indeed, a God Who loves us as if there were only one of us in the universe (Augustine). Instead of trying to foist commandments on young people and trying to drag them to church, we need first to introduce them to the Person of Jesus so that they may fall in love with Him. St. Isaac the Syrian speaks of becoming "drunk" with love for Jesus. If this happens, young people will want to come to church, and keeping the commandments will be a joy, not a burden.

"THOU"

It must be emphasized that a very important word in the Ten Commandments is the word "Thou," "Thou shalt...," "Thou shalt not..." God addresses each one of the commandments to us personally. He dignifies each one of us with a very personal "Thou." God is not giving these commandments to a mass of humanity. He is addressing you and no one else in a very pointed and personal way, "Thou, Mary, Jane, shalt...," "Thou, Nick, George, shalt not..."

We need to realize this because the Ten Commandments seem very cold and impersonal to people. This is because we do not hear the personal "Thou" addressed to us by God. We don't know the precious Lord Who is behind the commandments. All we hear is the dry letter of the law.

That is why we need first to be introduced and to come to know the Person of Jesus. We need to fall in love with Him.

AN EXAMPLE

Let me mention here the example of a young man who was born and raised in the Greek Orthodox Church, attended its Sunday School, participated in the liturgy as an altar boy and sang in the choir. But he never had an intimate and individual relationship with Christ. During college he was introduced to the work of the Holy Spirit through an evangelical campus group. Although he continued his sacramental participation in the Orthodox Church, he also attended an evangelical parish for its biblical teaching. After graduation, working with Campus Crusade for Christ put him in a situation to respond to his call for the priesthood in the Orthodox Church where he now serves with what he calls "a true and convert heart." This story, which has a nice ending, should serve as a sad reminder for Orthodox leaders, clergy and parents, about their many altar boys and Sunday School children, who leave the Church and never come back.

I shall let this priest speak for himself:

> *Like many who are born and raised within a*
> *particular Christian expression, I did not have a*
> *solid grasp of what it means to be a follower of*

3

Jesus Christ as a young person. In addition to the usual hurdles and perplexities confronting any young, twentieth-century Christian, I also faced a serious language barrier: the Orthodox parishes I participated in as a child held their service entirely in Greek. As with most Americans, I spoke only English.

During my high-school years I attended Sunday School, participated as an altar boy and sang in the choir (phonetically, of course). All of this experience gave me a closeness to my Eastern Orthodox heritage. Unfortunately, the one thing it did not give me was an intimate, understandable relationship with Jesus Christ. I am not saying He was absent from my life, or that I didn't know of Him. I did not, however, have an intimate communion or relationship with Him, in the words of Saint Ephraim, as "Lord and Master of my life.

NOT PAROCHIAL SCHOOLS

Fr. Andrew Greeley, a noted Roman Catholic sociologist, discovered that children who attend parochial schools and those who do not, are the same in the final analysis. Attending parochial school is no guarantee the child will not leave the Church. What really changes a person, he discovered, is not attending parochial school or confirmation classes, but the fact that there was someone in the child's life who loved him personally and unconditionally, and who himself had a personal relationship with God.

Here, then, is our great challenge: to make our Orthodox Christian faith personal first to ourselves and then to our young people!

Fr. Henri Nouwen once told a gathering of ministers, "Ministry is the least important thing. You cannot not minister if you are in communion with God. A lot of people are always concerned about: 'How can I help people? Or help the youth come to Christ? Or preach well?' But these are all basically nonissues. If you are burning with the love of Jesus, don't worry – everyone will know. They will say, 'I want to get close to

4

this person who is so full of God.'" If your faith is personal, it will be contagiously real.

CONTAGIOUSLY REAL

When as parents we teach our children, we should not teach just facts and traditions. We should share with them what our faith in Christ means to us personally. Sometimes we spend so much time teaching "about" Christ that we often miss the more important goal of helping our youngsters get to know Christ personally. There is a vast difference between learning about a person and actually meeting and knowing the person himself.

Many young people leave the Church because they are seeking a real, personal encounter with God which they have not found in their homes or churches. Let us listen for a moment as one of them speaks: "All I got at any church I ever went to were sermons or homilies about God, about the peace that passes understanding. Words, words, words! It was all up in the head. I never really felt it. It was all abstract, never direct, always somebody else's account of it. It was dull and boring. I'd sit or kneel or stand. I'd listen to or read prayers. But it seemed lifeless. It was like reading the label instead of eating the contents. But here (referring to one of the Eastern cults) it really happened to me. I experienced it myself. I don't have to take someone else's word for it."

I think there is much we can learn from the above statement. We need to share our Orthodox Christian faith in a very personal way with our children so that they come to experience for themselves the reality of the power, the presence, and the love of God in their lives.

Within the Muslim community, for example, those who become Christians do so because they have had a Christian friend, not because they lost a debate with a Christian preacher. It is the personal that attracts; it is the personal that saves.

Chapter Two

The God of Abraham, Isaac and Jacob

My God and my Lord, take me away from my
own self, and let me belong completely to
You.
My God and my Lord, take away everything
that keeps me apart from You.
My God and my Lord, grant me everything
that draws me closer to you.

– by a Church Father

THE GOD OF ABRAHAM, ISAAC AND JACOB

After meeting with Patriarch Alexei II about his Moscow Crusade, evangelist Billy Graham made the following statement:

The Russian Orthodox Church is unhappy about people proselytizing, but they don't mind preaching," said Graham. "The thing lacking in some Orthodox churches and teaching is a personal, daily relationship with Christ. This is what we'd like to do – not bring people out of the Orthodox church, but bring revival to it.

May I highlight the words, "The thing lacking in some Orthodox churches and teaching is a personal, daily relationship with Christ." We find the same problem, of course, in many non-Orthodox churches. People may know of Jesus, may even say they believe in Him, but they lack a daily, personal relationship with Him. How can anyone know someone without an I-Thou relationship with that person?

For anything to be real it has to be personal. If it does not become personal, it will not be real. This is especially true of our relationship with Christ. Yet what is a personal relationship with Christ, and how can we attain it?

GOD IS A PERSON

First of all, we must realize that God is a Person. God the Son is a Person. God the Holy Spirit is a Person. The Holy Spirit, for example, is not a "divine blast" as someone once described Him. He is not an "it." The Holy Spirit is a Person with Whom we can establish a personal I-Thou relationship. The word "Person," as applied to the Trinity, should help us understand that each person of the Trinity is Someone to Whom we can speak, of Whom we may make a request, Whom we can love, Whom we can praise, and with Whom we can establish a daily personal relationship.

GOD: PERSON OR THING?

When some people use the word God, they mean something like "the Principle of Creation" (Whitehead) or "life Force" (Bergson) or "Supreme Value" as if God were not personal but impersonal. They avoid

8

the idea of God as Someone and make Him Something, not *He* but *It*. When the Bible speaks of God, on the other hand, it uses personal catagories. God is pictured as Someone with Whom we can communicate; Someone Who addresses us and Whom we can address. We do *not* mean when we say that God is personal that He is a "person" like us, with arms, legs, hands, etc. We do mean that whatever else God is (and He is far greater than we can imagine), He is at *least* One with Whom we can establish a personal relationship. Since we cannot communicate with stones but only with persons, we say that God is personal.

ABRAHAM AND GOD

About 1900 years before Christ, God revealed Himself to a specific person: Abraham. God spoke to him and Abraham answered as we would answer any human person.

Christos Yannaras, an Orthodox theologian, writes, "The knowledge of God which arose from Abraham's personal encounter with God, has nothing to do with logical proofs. It was an experience of relationship only, and like every true relationship, it was based only on the faith or trust which is born between those who are in a relationship with one another... And Abraham trusted God, to the point of being ready to sacrifice the child whom Sarah had given him in her old age... God is neither an abstract concept nor an impersonal power. When the Hebrews speak about God, they say, 'The God of our fathers.' He is 'the God of Abraham, of Isaac, and of Jacob,' an actual person Whom their ancestors knew and with Whom they associated."[1]

If God is the "God of Abraham, Isaac and Jacob," then He is the God of persons; He is not the God of abstract values and principles. He is not the impersonal "Ground of all Being." Abraham, Isaac and Jacob are not abstract principles. They are persons whose lives are to be continued. Whoever joins the covenant of Abraham which is now fulfilled through Baptism in the new covenant, the new Israel, which is the Church, that person – who is baptized in the Church – is called to continue the life of Abraham, the life of complete faith and trust in God; the life of one who has a personal relationship with God as did Abraham. In a way, Abraham continues forever. We are Abraham, Isaac and Jacob; God's people who know God personally, love Him, trust Him, and follow Him.

---

1   "Elements of Faith," C. Yannaras. T&T Clark, Ltd. Edinburgh. 1991.

Let me say here that if God can be "the God of Jacob," who was one of the greatest connivers who ever lived, then there is real hope for you and me. If He can be Jacob's God then surely He can be my God, too. For I, too, am a sinner. Thus, because each of us is a person confronting a personal God, it follows that our relationship with Him must be personal.

"FACE TO FACE"

To see how personal our relationship to God can be, let us turn to Exodus 33:11:

> *Thus the Lord used to speak to Moses face to*
> *face, as a man speaks to his friend.*

In Exodus 6:7, we hear God speaking personally to His people, the Israelites, saying:

> *...and I will take you for my people, and I will*
> *be your God.*

In Deuteronomy 34:10 we catch another glimpse of how personal our relationship with God can be:

> *And there has not arisen a prophet since in*
> *Israel like Moses, whom the Lord knew face to*
> *face...*

Commenting on these Old Testament experiences with God, Dr. Christos Yannaras writes,

> *We have seen that from the beginning the*
> *experience of the patriarchs of Israel confirmed*
> *the personal character of the Divinity: They meet*
> *him 'person to person,' they speak with him 'face*
> *to face.' The God of Israel is the true God, that is,*
> *the really existing, living God, since He is the God*
> *of relationship, of personal immediacy.*[2]

But now we Christians have in store for us an even closer fellowship with the Lord than either Abraham or Moses had. The beloved Apostle

---

2   "Elements of Faith." C. Yannaras. T & T Clark, Ltd. Edinburgh. 1991.

John writes about each baptized Christian who truly follows Jesus: "When He [Christ] shall appear, we shall be like Him; for we shall see Him as He is" (I John 3:2). One day, as surely as sunset follows dawn, the Lord Jesus will return, and then we (you and I, with these very eyes) shall see Him face to face. That moment of recognition will change us into His glorious likeness. Because this glorious future awaits us, we are called to consider carefully now we ought to live here and now. For as St. John goes on to say, "Everyone who thus hopes in Him, purifies himself as He is pure" (I John 3:3).

It is to this kind of a "face to face," in Greek *prosopon pros prosopon* relationship to God that we are called.

Christos Yannaras continues,

> *He who gives us here and now such a wealth of life... has promised us also fullness of life, direct adoption, a face to face relationship with Him...*
>
> *How this new relationship with Him will operate, by means of what functions, I do not know. I merely rely on it. What I do know from such revelation of truth as He has given us is that the relationship will always be personal, that before Him, I will be me, as God knows me and loves me. I will be with my name and with the possibility of dialogue with Him, like Moses or Elijah on Mount Tabor. That is enough; perhaps it is more than enough.*[3]

Let me share with you this brief paragraph from a report submitted to Archbishop Iakovos in 1990 on the future of the Church. As you read, try to count how many times the word personal is used.

> *There can be no realization of the kingdom unless there is a personal response and a personal appropriation of God's saving, redeeming, and sanctifying grace. This goal is realized by the following: a personal faith commitment; personal and conscious participation in the Liturgy,*

3   "Elements of Faith." C. Yannaras. T & T Clark, Ltd. Edinburgh. 1991.

*worship and prayer; personal obedience to the
will of God; personal growth in love; personal
development of the image and likeness of God
within each of us toward Christ-likeness.*

A DOOR MUST BE ENTERED

Our relationship to Jesus must be personal if it is to be real. How can it be otherwise? Jesus is love – we must love Him as He loves us. He is Truth – we must accept His truth and experience it through obedience. He is Life – we must live Him. He is the Door – we must enter through Him. He is the Way – we must follow Him. He is the Word of God speaking to us; we must listen and obey Him. We do not get to know God by accumulating knowledge about Him found in books, but by knowing Him personally, loving Him, praying, obeying, and following.

St. John Climacus speaks of our love of God as "passionate": "Blessed is the person whose desire for God has become like the lover's passion for the beloved."

A story is told about William Jennings Bryan, that great American orator. As he was having his portrait painted, Bryan was asked, "Why do you wear your hair over your ears?" Bryan responded, "There is a romance connected with that. When I began courting Mrs. Bryan, she objected to the way my ears stood out. So, to please her, I let my hair grow to cover them." "But that was many years ago," the artist said. "Why don't you have your hair cut now?" "Because," Bryan winked, "the romance is still going on." Can that be said of you and me in our personal relationship with Christ?

THE GOSPEL OF PERSONAL ENCOUNTERS WITH JESUS

Fr. Raymond Brown states that the entire Gospel of John is a gospel of personal encounters with Jesus. One by one, Jesus encounters various people: Nicodemus, the Samaritan woman at the well, the cripple at Bethesda, the man born blind, Mary and Martha, and even Pilate. One by one they make their entrance onto the stage of John's gospel to encounter personally Jesus, the light of the world. And, in so doing, they judge themselves by whether or not they continue to come to the light or turn away and prefer darkness. Is it not the same with us? One by one we encounter in the darkness of the world Jesus, the Light. And our eternal destiny is decided by that personal encounter with the Light – whether we come to it or turn away to the darkness.

John Oxenham has written a beautiful poem expressing the personal aspect of our Christian faith:

Not what I believe, but whom!
Who walks beside me in the gloom?
Who shares the burden wearisome? Who all
the dim way does illumine,
And bids me look beyond the tomb
The larger life to live?

Not what do I believe.
But whom!
Not what
But whom!

I-THOU

Metropolitan Antonie of Transylvania writes,

God defined Himself saying: "I am who I am" (Exod 3:14). This definition reduces all attributes of God to the most primordial and ontological characteristics of His being. These characteristics are existence, being, possession of life, as opposed to non-existence, non-being, nothingness. We have here "He who is" vis-a-vis nothingness. On the Orthodox icons, in the image of Jesus Christ, the painters indicate His name and title on His halo with this short definition: O on: "He who is." From this divine name and attribute all other names and attributes are derived, and without these, all others have no meaning...

"He who is" is by this very definition a person, somebody who thinks, feels, loves and acts, a full personality who can establish relations with other persons, as an "I" in relation with "Thou" (Martin Buber).[4]

n Buber will always be known as the person who drew the
between the I, thou, and it, in relationship to other people. The
_____tionship means relating to people with the whole of our being.
It means genuine encounter, a reciprocal relationship which puts the I in
tune with life. The I-It relationship, on the other hand, implies treating
the other person not as a person but as an object, a thing to be used and
discarded.

Buber summed up his philosophy of life in these two sayings: "All
real living is meeting," and "In the beginning is the relationship." We
either meet the other person as a thou to whom we respond with our whole
personality (I-Thou), or we meet him as a thing to be used. That is the
I-It relationship. The I-Thou relationship is distinctively personal.

Vladimir Lossky said, "One prays to have the audacity and the
simplicity to say 'Thou' to God."[5] In the Lord's Prayer, Jesus gives us the
boldness to address God as "our Father," our "Daddy," Abba.

To relate to God as "Thou" is eternal life. Bishop Gerasimos
captured this thought when he wrote,

> *"Faith is not knowledge, but a meeting. Such
> a personal encounter with the divine and the
> eternal as seen in Christ will always be the highest
> and truest kind of knowledge that man can ever
> attain. This knowledge is eternal life" (Jn 17:3)*[6]

To know God is to relate to Him personally as "Thou." Metropolitan
Nicolae Corneanu writes, "Each 'I' longs for otherness, for a 'thou,' for
'us' – each 'I' longs ultimately for God. Ontologically, this feeling of
solitude cannot be satiated by human love, since it is rooted in man's
longing for God. It is, in fact, man's anguished longing for the divine
origin from which he arose and to which he shall return."

For Fr. Sophrony the fact that God revealed Himself to Moses as "I
am that I am" (Exodus 3:14) was like a Damascus road experience. He
wrote, "Great is the word 'I.' It designates the person. Only the person
truly lives... Because God says 'I,' man can say, 'thou.' In my 'I' and His
'thou' is found the whole of Being; both this world and God. Outside and

4   "Jesus Christ – The Life of the World." Ed. Ion Bria. WCC Publications. 1982.
5   "Orthodox Theology." SVS Press. 1978.
6   "Orthodox Faith and Life: Christ in the Gospels" Volume 1. HCO Press. 1980.

beyond Him, there is nothing. If I am in Him, then I too 'am'; but if I am outside Him, I die."[7]

In Orthodox theology we talk much about the incomprehensibility of the Divine Essence of God. We make "apophatic" statements about God – definitions of what God is not. We say that God is invisible (not visible), ineffable (not describable), eternal (not in time), infinite (not limited), immaterial (not material), etc. Yet Orthodox theology also emphasizes that this apophatic, incomprehensible God Who is Lord has willed to reveal Himself to us.

In revealing Himself to us, God did not merely give us some information about Himself, but He revealed His very self, His very person in Christ Jesus. This demands a personal response of love from us, a personal encounter, a personal relationship: I-Thou not I-It.

Commenting on the I-Thou response that God expects of us, Fr. Georges Florovsky wrote,

> *Not only in the Old but also in the New Testament we see not only God, but also man. We apprehend God approaching and appearing to man; and we see human persons who encounter God and listen attentively to His Word – and, what is more, respond to His words. We hear in Scripture also the voice of man, answering God in words of prayer or of thanksgiving or of praise. It is sufficient to mention the Psalms in this connection. And God desires, expects, and requires this response. God desires that man not only listens to His words, but that man also responds to them. God wants to involve man in 'conversation.'*[8]

---

7   "Sourozh" Number 59. February, 1995. Article by Maxime Egger. "Archimandrite Sophrony: A Man for the World."

8   "Creation and Redemption." Nordland Press. 1976.

Chapter Three

God Must be Experienced

Faith is a relation to God; belief is a relation to an idea or a dogma.

– Abraham Joshua Heschel

GOD MUST BE EXPERIENCED

God cannot be fully expressed. In fact, a God fully expressed is no God. God is too infinite to be fully expressed, but He can be experienced. God expressed Himself once in the Person of Jesus. The purpose of that expression was that He might be experienced personally in the lives of His people as Emmanuel – God with us. For, unless God becomes personal, He will not be real. When He does become personal to us, St. Isaac of Nineveh says that "We become inebriated with love for Him."

Plato belittled manual work and glorified mental work. In his "Republic" he put the philosophers in the highest position. Many followed him, insisting that only mental work is highly esteemed, until the experimental method came and showed the value of manual work in the laboratory. Later came John Dewey with his philosophy of Pragmatism in which he proved the value of direct experience. He believed that the best system of education is based upon direct experience, i.e., the person experiences truth by himself and gets in touch with the facts by himself. Recent trends in education have elaborated more upon the concept of experience. Man experiences truth in order to learn truth, existentially and experientially. Experience is not limited to individual experience. There is also a collective experience. In the Orthodox Church we have Sacred Tradition, which is the collective experience of the Church through the centuries under the guidance of the Holy Spirit.

The call of modern thought to man is to enter into experience in order to learn. And this is the call of God from ancient times: "Taste and see that the Lord is good." The hymns of the Church are highly personal and existential. "Today Christ is born..." "Today His body is suspended on the cross..." "Today... Today..." What is this but an invitation to experience personally Christmas, Good Friday, Pascha, the Ascension, Pentecost – to experience them personally as if they were happening now, to me, today.

THE LITURGICAL YEAR: A LIVING AND PERSONAL ENCOUNTER WITH JESUS

The liturgical year not only re-enacts the great saving events in the life of Jesus, but also places us in each event in a very personal way. An existential encounter takes place between us and Christ in the events of His birth, crucifixion, resurrection, etc. These sacred events are mystically present in the Church here and now. We re-enter each event in such a way that it becomes a unique and refreshingly new act of salvation for us today. Thus, far from being a cold and lifeless representation of the events of the past, the liturgical year is a living and personal encounter with Jesus today. Today He comes to be born in the manger of my soul and yours to bring us new life. Today He offers me His precious Body and Blood for my salvation. Today He hangs on the cross for me. Today He is resurrected and I am resurrected with Him. Today He is transfigured and I am transfigured with Him. Today He ascends into heaven and I ascend with Him. So it is that the beautiful word *today* tears down the walls of the past and the future and makes Christ the eternally present One, Who is "the same yesterday and today and forever" (Hebr. 13:8).

Each year the liturgical calendar relives and makes present again the sacred events of our salvation so that we are there personally when they happen. The past reaches out and joins the present. The acts of God for His people are not buried in the past. They live in the present. History does not exhaust grace. God is present through the centuries. He never ceases accomplishing the work He has begun.

FAITH: A PERSONAL ENCOUNTER

Faith is never mere intellectual assent or blind submission; it is the fidelity of a person to a Person. It is a relationship, a meeting, a personal encounter with the living Lord Jesus. It is a living, personal, saving relationship with Jesus, Who is my Lord and my God. Abraham talked with God, person to person, as a friend to a friend. Moses did so "face to face."

Through the power of the Holy Spirit in His Body, the Church, we too can have a deeply dynamic personal relationship with Jesus Christ, the God-Man. We can experience Him as a God of love.

We need to accept Jesus as Lord and Savior of our lives not just once, as in some "born again" experience, but every day, as we do when we confess Him in the Nicene Creed. Every day we need to affirm that Jesus Christ is our Savior and the Lord of our lives, that His suffering, death, and resurrection have meaning for us today, that what He teaches and offers in the Bible and in the Church is for us to accept, experience, and obey today.

19

ST. SYMEON AND THE CHRIST CHILD

When Symeon saw the Theotokos bringing the baby Jesus to the Temple on the 40th day, inspired by the Holy Spirit, he recognized Jesus as the Messiah, and taking Jesus in his arms, he prayed,

> *Lord, now let thy servant depart in peace*
> *according to your word; for my eyes have seen*
> *your salvation which You have prepared in the*
> *presence of all people, a light for revelation to*
> *the Gentiles, and for glory of your people Israel.*
> *– Luke 2:29-32*

Commenting on Symeon's famous prayer, Bishop Gerasimos has written, "This (prayer) of Symeon is repeated by our Church at the end of every Vesper Service, and by the priest to himself at the end of every liturgy to reassure us that in going to church and in worship we have seen with the eyes of our soul the Savior Lord; we have talked with Him. After that experience, we leave filled with peace and spiritual joy. We can consider our church attendance a failure if we do not experience this emotion."[9] Just as Symeon saw Jesus and held Him in His arms, we, too, can experience His presence personally in prayer and in the worship services of the Church. Through the Eucharist we can take Jesus in our arms and embrace Him as did Symeon. Unless our faith is as personal as that, it will not be real.

What is more joyful than an encounter, a meeting with someone we love? To truly live is to look forward, to anticipate. What are we anticipating? What are we waiting for? Are we, like Symeon, anticipating, waiting, pondering, praying for our ultimate meeting with God? If we are, then we, too, shall experience Symeon's joy: "Let me now depart. I have seen the light of revelation in the face of Jesus. I have met the Child Who has brought God's salvation, His love, and peace to the world. I am fulfilled and ready to leave this world."

Fr. Alexander Schmemann wrote the following about how deeply personal our Christian faith must be:

> *Faith, in its very nature and essence, is*
> *something deeply personal, and therefore it is only*

---

9   "Orthodoxy: Faith and Life: Christ in the Gospels." HCO Press. 1980.

really alive when seen in the context of personal experience. Only when a particular teaching of the Church – or, as we say, a dogma, an affirmation of some particular truth – becomes my faith and my experience, and therefore the main content of my life, does this faith come alive. If one reflects on faith and thinks about how it passes from one person to another, it becomes obvious that what really convinces, inspires and converts is personal experience. This is especially important in Christianity, because in its essence, Christian faith is a personal encounter with Christ, an acceptance not of this or that teaching or dogma about Christ, but of Christ Himself. In other terms, Christianity is extremely personal. This in no way implies that it is individualistic, for all believers encounter, recognize and love exactly one and the same Christ. But Christ addresses Himself to each person, so that each faith is at the same time unique.[10]

If a friendship does not grow it will stagnate and die. So, too, our relationship with Jesus. Unless we daily try to grow closer to Him, we will find ourselves falling into indifference, or possibly losing our faith in Him altogether. As Christians we must always strive to know Christ Jesus, to know Him personally as one person knows another. If some people complain that Orthodoxy is too abstract, it is because they do not really know Jesus in a personal way.

I AM THE VINE, YOU ARE THE BRANCHES

For Orthodox Christians, religion is a relationship with God in the Person of Jesus. It is on this personal relationship to Jesus that the happiness and the purposefulness of life depends. And it shall be on the basis of this relationship to Christ that our eternal destiny shall be decided. Jesus is the door Who leads us to the Father and the Holy Spirit.

---

10   "Celebration of Faith." Volume 1. A. Schmemann. SVS Press. Crestwood, NY.

What kind of a relationship do we have to Jesus? Is it a relationship that is kept alive through faith, prayer, the sacraments and obedience to His commandments? Or is it a relationship kept dead by sin and indifference? It was concerning this relationship that Jesus said, "I am the vine, you are the branches. He who abides in me and I in him, he it is that bears much fruit, for apart from me you can do nothing. If a man does not abide in me, he is cast forth as a branch and withers... If you abide in me, and my words abide in you, ask whatever you will and it shall be done for you" (John 15, 5-8).

THE CHURCH FATHERS: ST. SYMEON THE NEW THEOLOGIAN

One of the Church Fathers who greatly emphasized the personal aspect of faith was St. Symeon the New Theologian. He emphasized that the Christian life must be more than a routine observance of a rule, however strict that rule and exact its observance. To be at all meaningful there must be in the Christian life, says St. Symeon, the personal experience of the presence and the power of the living Christ. To reinforce his point, Symeon was not afraid to use his own personal experience of conversion and illumination. He would say that just as a pregnant woman knows there is a child within her, so every Christian should know and be able to experience the presence of God within. It has been said that many of the Greek Fathers theologized from their experience of God in His Scriptural Word.

Of course, St. Symeon raised a storm of controversy in the Church as he challenged the religious formalism of his time. But this did not prevent the Orthodox Church from canonizing him and applying to him the great title of "the New Theologian," thus placing him in the same category as St. John the Divine and St. Gregory of Nazianzus, who were both named "the Theologian."

Let me quote from one of Symeon's teachings to his monks:

> *Prayer is conversation directly with God,
> being always with God, having one's soul united
> with him and one's mind inseparable, as David
> says: "My soul clings to you" (Ps 62:9) and "My
> soul thirsts for you" (Ps 62:3); "As the deer longs
> for the springs of water, so my soul longs for you,*

22

O God" (Ps 121:1); "I will love you, O God my strength" (Ps 16:2); "My soul is always in your hands" (Ps 118:109).

Speaking on how attentive we should be during the Divine Liturgy, St. Symeon writes, "Stand with trembling as if you were seeing the Son of God being sacrificed before you."

Daniel B. Clendenin explains St. Symeon's personal approach to God as follows:

> *Of all the Orthodox fathers who viewed the life of theological reflection as intensely practical mystical communion with the living God, few stand out more than Saint Simeon the New Theologian. For Simeon, a conscious awareness of the indwelling Holy Spirit was the necessary sign of true Christian identity. It would be no exaggeration to think of him as a charismatic theologian in terms of both his personality and his doctrine. Throughout his writings, including his accounts of his own visions of God, Simeon stresses the idea of God as mystical light. Simeon's entire purpose is to lead his reader into a direct experience of the living God, Who is light, an experience in which "one has to destroy idols, go beyond words and ideas, and live in the awesome darkness of mystery that becomes a light to those who have become purified." That is, Simeon leads us from the darkness of the apophatic mystery of God to the light of mystical union with Him.!11•*

The very personal relationship St. Symeon had with Jesus is demonstrated in the following dialogue he had with Jesus in a vision: "Are you my God?" The answer was, "Yes, I am the God who became man for you. Because you desired me and sought after me with all your soul, you will henceforth be my brother, my friend, and the co-inheritor of my glory."

---

11   "Eastern Orthodox Christianity: A Western Perspective." D.B. Clendenin. Baker Books. 1994.

Elisabeth Behr-Sigel describes St. Symeon's personal approach to Jesus and the Holy Spirit as follows:

Symeon characteristically insisted on the indwelling of the Holy Spirit in every baptized person, and we can rightly underscore the Christocentric nature of his piety, of his "deeply tender feelings" for Jesus, as the Monk of the Eastern Church has said. But this intimate relation with Christ was for him inseparable from the living experience of the gift of the Holy Spirit. Even though Symeon loved Christ deeply, he was also the herald, the announcer, of the outpouring of the Holy Spirit which he called upon all baptized people to make real in their lives. We must take possession of the Spirit whom we have received in baptism so as to become conscious, in him, of the fact that we have truly been reclothed by Christ. In His catechetical instructions, Symeon the hegumen of St. Mamas never tired of exhorting his listeners to "become conscious of these things." His doctrine stated that "mystical experience is necessary for everyone" and was essentially a call to take personal possession of grace and an insistence on illumination by the Spirit. Every Christian, by virtue of his baptism, is called upon to aspire to this illumination. Symeon proclaimed that eternal life begins here and now and that we must know it and gain knowledge of it through experience.

"If we claim that all this is accomplished in a hidden and unconscious way, so that we are not in the slightest way aware of what has happened, then what makes us different from dead bodies?" [12]

---

12 "The Place of the Heart." Elisabeth Behr-Sigel. Oakwood Publications. Torrance, CA. Translated by Fr. Stephen Bigham. 1991. Page 91.

ST. ANTHONY

A great saint whose whole life changed when he applied God's word personally to his life was St. Anthony. St. Athanasius tells the story:

> *Antony was a rich young fellow, born into a Christian family in Egypt. His parents died when he was just entering his teens; their large estate fell to him. He grew up fast, carrying that responsibility. He had all the money in the world and all the cares too.*

> "In Church one Sunday the Scripture reading came from Christ's reply to the rich young ruler: 'If you want to be perfect, go, sell your possessions and give to the poor, and you will have treasure in heaven. Then come, follow me.'
> "Something in that familiar passage hit Antony. It was as though Jesus had given those words directly to him, personally, that very moment. Antony didn't even wait for the service to end. He rushed out of the church and set about preparing his records so that his property could be sold and the profit distributed to the poor.

> "From that day, Antony devoted his live to prayer. He went to live in a hut on the edge of town, farming to keep himself alive. Fifteen years later he moved into the desert."

Anthony was followed by many other monks, or anchorites, who withdrew from the sinful society of their day to find salvation in personal, one-to-one encounters with God in the desert.

ST. GREGORY NAZIANZUS

Another Church Father, St. Gregory of Nazianzus, speaks of Jesus very personally:

> *I share everything with Christ, spirit and body, nails and resurrection.*

Christ... Thou art for me my native land, my strength, my glory, everything.

Christ is my strength and my breath and the wonderful prize for my running.

It is He Who enables me to run well.

I love Him as my purest love because for those whom He loves He is faithful beyond all that we can conceive.

In Him is my joy even if He chooses to send me some suffering, because I aspire to be purified as gold in the fire.

ST. TIKHON

Listen to the beautifully personal way that St. Tikhon, a Russian saint of the 18th century, prays to God:

Listen, my soul: God has come to us;
Our Lord has visited us.
For my sake He was born of the Virgin Mary,
He was wrapped in swaddling clothes,
He who covers heaven with the clouds
*   and vests Himself with robes of light.*
For my sake He was placed in the lowly manger,
He whose throne is the heavens and whose feet
*   rest upon earth.*
For my sake He was fed with His mother's milk,
He who feeds all creatures.
For my sake He was held in His mother's arms,
He who is borne by the Cherubim
*   and holds all creatures in His embrace.*
For my sake He was circumcised according to
*   the law,*
He who is maker of the Law.
For my sake, He who is unseen became visible
*   and lived among men,*
He who is my God.
My God became one like me, like a man;

the word became flesh,
and my Lord, the Lord of Glory,
took for my sake the form of a servant
and lived upon earth and walked upon earth
He who is the King of Heaven.

According to St. Tikhon every Christian has the right to say, "For my sake God created the world. For me He became man in Christ. For me He suffered on the cross. For me He rose from the dead and ascended to heaven."

ST. JOHN CHRYSOSTOM

In describing the creation of the world, St. John Chrysostom personalizes it by saying:

> *The creation is beautiful and harmonious, and God has made it all just for your sake.*
>
> *He has made it beautiful, grand, varied, rich. He has made it capable of satisfying all your needs, to nourish your body and also to develop the life of your soul by leading it towards the knowledge of himself – all this, for your sake.*
>
> *For your sake he has made the sky beautiful with stars. He has embellished it with sun and moon for your sake, so that you can take pleasure in it and profit by it.*

FROM "THE WAY OF A PILGRIM"

The pilgrim in "The Way of a Pilgrim" describes how he experienced God's presence as a result of praying the Jesus Prayer:

> *Sometimes, there was such a bubbling up in my heart and a lightness, a freedom, a joy so great that I was transformed and felt in ecstasy. Sometimes I felt a burning love for Jesus Christ and for the whole divine creation. Sometimes, my tears flowed all on their own in thanksgiving to the Lord Who had mercy on me, such a hardened*

sinner. Sometimes, my limited mind was illuminated.... Sometimes the sweet warmth of my heart spilled over into all my being, and I felt the presence of the Lord with great emotion. Sometimes, I felt a powerful and deep joy on invoking the name of Jesus Christ, and I understood the meaning of His saying, "The Kingdom of God is within you."

THE NEED TO EXPERIENCE TRUTH

People hunger to do more than just believe the right things. There is a hunger for some experience of God in their lives. This is what Orthodox Christianity has always offered: not only intellectual understanding but a spiritual experience of the living God. Sts. Symeon the New Theologian, Gregory Palamas, John Climacus and others defend the legitimacy and even necessity of direct experience with God. In the Philokalia itself, theology is understood less in terms of intellectual understanding and more as a level of spiritual experience. We Orthodox learn our theology not just from books but more especially from the liturgy, from prayer, from hysychia (silence), and from the Jesus Prayer. Writing on the importance of experiencing truth, St. John Climacus says:

Do you imagine plain words can precisely or truly or appropriately describe the love of the Lord... and assurance of the heart? Do you imagine that talk of such matters will mean anything to someone who has never experienced them? If you think so, then you will be like a man who with words and examples tries to convey the sweetness of honey to people who have never tasted it. He talks uselessly. Indeed I would say he is simply prattling.

NOT AN INTELLECTUAL ASSENT BUT A LIVING REALITY

One of our problems is that we may know of God's love intellectually, but most of us fail to experience it, to know it deep down in our hearts. When we do come to know God's love personally, our whole life changes. Someone said, "For each of us the day on which we realize that our Lord loves us personally and individually is a red-letter day, a kind of spiritual birthday."

One person said, "It had been my belief that God loved all of mankind, but I found it much more difficult to comprehend that He loved me personally. It finally became a reality through my own son when he was very small. One night as I stood looking down on my sleeping child, my love for him seemed to reach out and fill the whole room; I experienced an overwhelming sense of joy. Instinctively my spirit rose in thanksgiving to God for the gift of our son and our joy in him.

"At this moment there dawned upon my consciousness the certainty that God loved me like that – only much, much more. The assurance of His love ceased to be just an intellectual assent and became a living reality. It was then that I began to understand something of my own worth in the eyes of God, and through this recognition I found a new and growing capacity to love."

Diadochus of Photike wrote,

> *We do not readily despise the delights of this life*
> *if we do not taste with complete satisfaction the*
> *sweetness of God.*

Chapter Four

To Know God Personally

Evolution is impersonal. You cannot tell your child, "Evolution loves you," but you can say, "Jesus loves you."

TO KNOW GOD PERSONALLY

"To know" can mean different things to different people. Ask the man in the street if he knows the president of the United States, and he will say yes. That does not mean that he knows him personally; he has probably never seen him personally. But it means that he is acquainted with who the president is.

To be acquainted with who God may be is a start but nothing more. To know Him in a personal way is what is needed. In the Old Testament the verb "to know" meant such intimacy of relationship that it was often used to describe conjugal relations between husband and wife. "Adam knew Eve... and begat Cain."

Clearly, to know God means not to know about Him but to know Him intimately and personally. How does one get to know God personally? The answer is by experiencing God through faith, commitment, prayer, repentance, silence, the sacraments, the Jesus Prayer, and His word. God can and does make His presence felt. He can and does speak to you in the silence of your soul. He can and does warm and thrill you until you no longer doubt that He is near. You cannot force such experience from God. He gives it freely. He gave it to Abraham, Moses and the saints. There is not one to whom God refuses His closer presence. But you have to ask... and ask... and ask. Seek... and seek... and seek. Knock... and knock... and knock. You have to be persistent and be willing to spend time with Him.

St. John Chrysostom depicts Christ as personally imploring our love:

Who can be more generous than I? I am father,
I am brother, I am spouse, as well as food,
clothing, home, root, foundation, everything you
could wish for. You need nothing else. I will
even become your servant for I came to serve,
not to be served. I am also friend, member,
head, brother, sister, mother. I am everything to
you. You have only to be my friend. I became
poor for your sake, a beggar for your sake; I
was crucified for you, buried for you. In heaven
I implore the Father for you. You have become
everything for me – brother, co-heir, friend,
member. What more can you desire?

FOUR BOOKS FOR HEAVEN

It has been said that it takes four books to get us to heaven. We can easily guess what the first two are: the Bible and the Prayerbook. The last two are not as well known but equally as important, i.e., the datebook and the checkbook. The datebook is important because it shows how much time we actually spend with God in prayer, in the liturgy, in diaconia and service to the needy. The checkbook, of course, shows how many of our financial resources we are investing in the work of the kingdom. In the words of Jesus, our heart will always be where our treasure lies. If our faith is personal, it will be real, and it will reveal itself in these four books.

Faith is not something that must be intellectually understood as much as it is something that must be experienced and lived. It will find expression in every area of life. It is, in its deepest essence, a living relationship of love with God in, with, and through His Son, Jesus.

St. Gregory of Sinai explains that only those who participate in truth can know truth:

> *He who seeks to understand commandments*
> *without fulfilling commandments, and to*
> *acquire such understanding through learning*
> *and reading, is like a man who takes a shadow*
> *for truth. For the understanding of truth is given*
> *to those who have become participants in truth*
> *(who have tasted it through living). Those who*
> *are not participants in truth and are not*
> *initiated therein, when they seek this*
> *understanding, draw it from a distorted wisdom.*
> *Of such men the Apostle says: "the natural man*
> *receiveth not the things of the Spirit" (I Cor. II.*
> *14) even though they boast of their knowledge*
> *of truth.*

Fr. Schmemann said once, "We cannot have trust in someone whom we know only superficially. We must know this someone, we must have created a relationship with him. In the end it is necessary to love this someone in order to have confidence in him.

"Our knowledge of God does not come from books, nor is it the result of reflection. To arrive at knowledge of God, it is necessary to cultivate a relationship with Him. We do not know God as an idea, as the result of a process of thought. It is something else entirely: God is known through an immediate relationship, and it is this which we must seek."

HOW DOES ONE EXPERIENCE GOD?

The big question is HOW? How does one experience God in life? The answer is through the commitment and surrender of one's life to Jesus, by speaking to Him every day in prayer, by turning to Him for guidance and strength, by reading daily His personal love letter, the Holy Bible, by praying for and receiving the Gift of the Holy Spirit, by receiving Him in the Sacrament of Communion.

In some Orthodox churches in the Middle East, I have seen an object resembling an ostrich egg suspended immediately above the flickering flame of hanging votive lights. The symbolism of the ostrich egg has to do with the heat produced by the flame of the votive candle. Just as an ostrich must sit on the egg for a long time in order to slowly hatch it with the heat of its body, so the Christian must remain close to the flame of Christ. He must stay close to the church and must nurture his faith through daily prayer and regular communion with Christ through the Eucharist. Only then will faith grow, develop, mature and come to life. The ostrich egg represents the embryonic state of faith which can spring to life through patient and faithful ascesis, producing a life full of the fruits of the Spirit, a life that will glorify the Trinity.

LORD, DO I REALLY KNOW YOU?

An anonymous monk of the Eastern Church has written, "Jesus charged Peter, who gave a sound answer and confessed the Messias, not to reveal the mystery publicly (Matthew 16:13-20). Every person has to discover for himself the secret of Jesus. And even if we learn from others who Jesus is, and even if the others are commissioned to teach this to us, it is only by an intensely personal experience that we shall come to know who Jesus is.

"In fact, of the many souls who believed all they must believe, and who led a just and pious life, we may wonder: did this soul know the Saviour? Did he know him intimately... as a man and woman who love each other can know each other...? A number of acquired notions (and also true ones) concerning the Saviour are often substituted for a personal

34

and intense knowledge of the Saviour. It can be a hindrance just like a screen between Jesus and us. Lord, do I really know You, or do I only know what I have read about You, what I have heard about You?"[13]

BOTH PERSONAL AND COMMUNAL

Our Orthodox Christian faith is anchored in a personal relationship with God. God is not a machine but a Person with Whom we can establish a daily personal relationship. It is a relationship that is nurtured and nourished by our membership in the Body of Christ, the Church. It is not a "Lone Ranger" type of relationship. It is a relationship that grows out of our being connected with Christ in His Body, the Church, and through the grace we receive from prayer and the sacraments, especially the Eucharist.

Our relationship to God is both communal and personal. But we often lose the communal because we live in a society that is radically individualistic. We need to remember that our personal relationship with Christ is anchored and rooted in the communal relationship we have with Him as members of His Body, the Church. Of course, we can also lose the personal in the communal (just coming to church once in a while but having no personal relationship with Jesus). We need both! We need both private prayer at home and communal prayer in Church. The one feeds the other.

Fr. Georges Florovsky expressed this well when he wrote, "One is saved only in community, and yet salvation is mediated always through personal faith and obedience."

APRON-STRING RELIGION

This means that there is no such thing as an "apron-string" religion. Some people assume that because their mother has a personal and living faith, she's going to heaven. And if they hold on to her apron strings, they believe they'll get there too. But it is not enough to have a godly person for an ancestor, even if it's Abraham himself. Genes may run in a family but not faith. Of course, it's a wonderful privilege to have believing parents and a long tradition of godly ancestors, but you're wasting the privilege if you are not able to confess personally "I believe..." and if

---

13   "Jesus: A Dialogue With the Saviour" by a Monk of the Eastern Church. Desclee Co., Inc.

following your baptism, you have not made a personal confession of faith in Jesus as Lord, which (confession), of course, is renewed in every liturgy when you confess the Creed, and when you pray the pre-Communion prayer, "I believe and confess that You are the Christ, the Son of the Living God..."

MY GOD

"Religion is a matter of personal pronouns," someone said, "I, being able to say to God, 'My God,' and I, knowing that God says to me, 'My child.'"

For the saints of the Church, such as St. Paul, St. Jerome, St. Symeon the New Theologian, and so many others, Jesus was an intensely real person with whom it was possible to establish a profoundly personal relationship. We can catch a small glimpse of this in the many instances where the Saints and Fathers of the Church refer to Jesus not simply as "Jesus" but as "my Jesus," a phrase that betrays a wonderful sense of intimacy. St. Paul speaks of Jesus as the one who "loved me and gave Himself for me."

UNTO YOU IS BORN

We read in Scripture concerning the birth of Jesus, "Unto you is born this day in the city of David, a Savior, who is Christ the Lord." Mark these words, "Unto you..." It is not simply to humanity in general that Jesus comes, it is to each one of us personally that He comes. He desires to be your Savior in a way that is unique, entirely personal and exceptional.

The Word is continually being born in the stable of our heart. As Angelus Silesius wrote, "Even if Christ were to be born a thousand times at Bethlehem, if He is not born in you, you are lost for eternity."

Eternal life is meant to start right here on earth when we welcome Jesus into the stable of our heart and develop a daily personal relationship with Him as living members of His Body, the Church.

Bishop Kallistos Ware emphasizes the deeply personal aspect of our Orthodox faith when he writes,

> *Because of the Comforter's (the Holy Spirit's)*
> *presence in our heart, we do not simply know*
> *Christ at fourth or fifth hand, as a distant figure*

*from long ago, about whom we possess factual
information through written records; but we
know Him directly here and now, in the present,
as our personal Savior and our Friend. With the
Apostle Thomas we can affirm, "My Lord and
my God" (Jn. 20-28). We do not merely say,
"Christ died," but "Christ died for me." We do
not merely say, Christ rose, but "Christ is
risen" – He lives now, for me and in me. This
relationship with Jesus is precisely the work of
the Spirit.*[14]

WITH CHRIST

Perhaps no one expresses the personal aspect of our Orthodox faith better than St. Paul. He uses several compound verbs that begin with the Greek preposition syn (with): "I suffer with Christ... I am crucified with Christ... I die with Christ... I am buried with Christ... I am raised and live with Christ. I am carried off to heaven and sit at the right hand of the Father with Christ" (Rom 6:3-11, Gal 2:20, 2 Cor 1:5, 4:7, Col 2:20, Eph 2:5-6). This is Paul's way of underscoring the importance of our personal participation in redemption by "putting on Christ" and assimilating Him. "I live, yet not I, but Christ lives in me."

St. Gregory of Nazianzus expressed it this way:

*Yesterday I was crucified with Christ; today I am
glorified with Him.*

*Yesterday I was dead with Him; today I am shar-
ing in His resurrection.*

*Yesterday I was buried with Him; today I am
waking with Him from the sleep of death.*

HOW FAR HE WILL GO FOR US

In the Person of Jesus Christ we can see just how far God is willing to run to lead us back from the brink. Christ came all the way down from heaven for us. He became a slave for us even to the point of washing our

---

14   "The Orthodox Way," Kallistos Ware. SVS Press. Crestwood, NY. 1979.

lying the death of a slave on the cross for our sins. He came
.........ng after His people in this fallen world, calling us back to the
Father's house. He even "descended into hell" in order to bring us back
to the Father. As St. John Chrysostom says He "did not cease doing
everything until He led us into heaven." He looks at us today, beckoning
us to come with open arms as He says, "I want to gather you together as
a hen gathers her brood under her wings." How sad that so often He has
to add those terrible words, "But you would not come."

All of God's love is for you! It is uniquely personal. His sacrifice
on the cross is for you! His death and resurrection are for you, for your
sin, your guilt, your inner restlessness, your forgiveness, your peace. He
comes after you even now as you read this message. He opens His arms
and His heart to you. He wants to be part of your life to help bear your
burdens and guide you on the way to heaven.

WHEN REAL LIFE BEGINS

Go through history, pick out some of the great spiritual giants and
ask them, "When did you really begin to live?" And one by one they will
give you the same answer, "When I met Jesus Christ." Whether it be
Zacchaeus or St. Paul or St. Augustine or any one of the saints, the answer
is the same, "I began to live – really live – when I met Christ personally,
when I became aware of His love for me and submitted my life to Him."

Why did God choose to come into the world as a baby? Simply
because everybody loves babies! And God wants to be loved by you and
by me. Three times He asks Peter, "Do you love me?" He wants to be
loved just as He loves you. He came to earth at Christmas to tell you,
"You are my beloved son or daughter. I love you!" There is no greater
message than this unconditional love of God. This is what the gospel is
all about. Believe it, and your live cannot but be changed.

The name given to Jesus is "Emmanuel," which means "God with
us." God with me! God with you! What this really means is that God has
time for me. God has time for you. He has time for us because He loves
us. The question is: Do we have time for Him?

The essence of Christianity is a love relationship with God. The
more we love God, the more we will love to do His will, to pray, to serve,
to obey, to follow.

GET THE MONKEYS OFF YOUR BACK

The trouble with many of us is that we are empty inside, and we're trying to fill the inner emptiness with things. Henri Nouwen says that we are like a banana tree filled with monkeys. Our problem is one of trying to get the monkeys off our back, to create a little space inside so God can come and tell us, "I love you. You belong to me. You are my beloved son or daughter." So we keep trying to get the monkeys off our backs by keeping some space open for God, some quiet time each day for prayer and meditation, and for the liturgy on Sunday, so we can hear the voice of God as it tries to get through to us with God's personal love: "You are my beloved son or daughter. I created you out of nothing. I redeemed you with the blood of my only begotten Son, Jesus. I sealed you with the gift of the Holy Spirit. I want you to be with me in heaven to behold my glory. You belong to me. "

God's deeply personal love for us is expressed by Thomas A. Kempis in the following prayer:

LOVE SO DEEP, SO HIGH, SO BROAD

O Love, how deep, how broad, how high,
O great, O wondrous mystery,
That God, the Son of God, should take
Our mortal form for mortals' sake!

> *He sent no angel to our race,*
> *Of higher or of lower place,*
> *But He Himself to this world came*
> *And wore the robe of human frame.*

For us baptized! then Spirit-led
He fasted – who the thousands fed;
For us temptations sharp He knew,
For us the Tempter overthrew.

> *For us He prayed, for us He taught,*
> *For us His ev'ry work He wrought.*
> *By words, and signs, and actions, thus*
> *Still seeking not Himself, but us.*

For us to wicked men betrayed,
Scourged, mocked, in crown of thorns arrayed;
For us at length gave up His breath.

    For us He rose from death again,
    For us He went on high to reign,
    For us He sent His Spirit here
    To guide, to strengthen, and to cheer.

All glory to our Lord and God
For love so deep, so high, so broad;
The Trinity whom we adore
Forever and forevermore.

    – Attributed to Thomas A. Kempis, 1380-11471
    – translated by Benjamin Webb, 1820-1885

Chapter Five

What is
Church Membership?

Orthodoxy is the Church of Christ on earth.
The Church of Christ is not an institution; it
is a new life with Christ and in Christ,
guided by the Holy Spirit."

– Sergius Bulgakov

WHAT IS CHURCH MEMBERSHIP?

What is church membership? Is it being baptized? Is it paying one's fair share? Is it being born into a church? Is it a building I sometimes go to? Or is it a personal relationship with Jesus as "my Lord and my God?" Of course, it is the latter. When we were baptized we were asked to renounce Satan and to accept Christ. We were asked, "Do you accept Jesus? Do you believe in Jesus as King and God?" At baptism we established a personal relationship with Jesus. Church membership, therefore, is a personal relationship with Jesus which takes place and is nourished in the context of the Church, the Body of Christ, through faith, prayer, commitment, worship and the sacraments.

We are not saved by being members of a building we call "church." And we do not pay "dues" to the Church, since it is not a "club." The church is a Person. It is Christ – His very Body. We receive life from being attached not to a building but to a Person, and by being in a living and loving relationship with that Person. Jesus did not come to establish an abstract impersonal institution or religion. He came to offer Himself, God in Person, living and dwelling in our hearts through faith.

NOT BY INHERITANCE

For too many of us religion has come by inheritance. We have never said to God as Job did, "I had heard of You, Lord, by the hearing of the ear, but now I have seen You." In other words, "Now I have seen You with my own eyes. Now I know you personally."

Most of us have become disciples of the disciples of the disciples of someone in the past who had personally experienced God. But it is impossible to transmit real love or commitment this way.

For many people the Christian faith is a secondhand faith inherited from their parents. But some things cannot be inherited. Real estate can, money can, but not prayer, not faith, not commitment, not the kingdom of God. All the prayers of others in the past cannot redeem anyone who cannot say as did the blind man who was healed by Jesus, "One thing I know, that, whereas I was blind, now I see." Goethe said once, "The possessions which you have inherited from your ancestors – earn them in order truly to own them." If faith is not personal, it will not be real.

MATCHING THE SAINTS?

Often we are overwhelmed by the feats of the great saints of the Church. How can we match what they did? But we are not called to match what they did. Each of us is uniquely different and special. We are called to live according to our unique situation with the special talents God has given us. Nobody expressed this better than Evagrius:

> *Likewise anyone who wishes to embark on the labours of the virtuous life should train himself gently, until he finally reaches the perfect state. Do not be perplexed by the many paths trodden by our Fathers of old, each different from the other; do not zealously try to imitate them all: this would only upset your way of life. Rather, choose a way of life that suits your feeble state; travel on that, and you will live, for your Lord is merciful and he will receive you, not because of your achievements, but because of your intentions, just as he received the destitute woman's gift.*

We read in the book, "Come and See," edited by Father Theodore Bobosh:

> *What is missing is a living, "practiced" Christian faith to go along with the strong doctrinal correctness of the Orthodox Church. It is quite difficult to believe that the ordinary Orthodox Christian has any personal knowledge of or relationship with God at all. Certainly, outside of the services there is very little direct or enthusiastic discussion of Christ and His Church among the ordinary (i.e., non-clerical) folk. And the extent of the Orthodox Christian's ignorance concerning his own faith (not to mention the faiths of other Americans) is both incredible and alarming. Too many are depending passively upon the historic "orthodoxy" of the Church. Too many are trying to live, not by their own personal faith in Christ, but by the "faith of our fathers."*

Before the plane takes off we are told that if anything happens, we are to put our own oxygen mask on first, then that of our children. If we do not have a personal faith; if we ourselves as parents, priests, teachers, have not put on Christ first, then we cannot pass Him on to others. We cannot help save others, if we ourselves are not saved. We must put on Christ first before we can share Him with others.

GRACE AND DISCIPLESHIP

A noted Orthodox theologian, Fr. George Dragas, wrote, "Looked at from the side of God, theology is grace, the grace of the Trinity. From the side of man, it is costly discipleship." Our response to God's grace is discipleship. It is the discipleship of nourishing and developing a daily personal relationship with God. Eternal life begins now with a daily, personal relationship with Jesus lived out in His Body – the Church.

A book that will help you greatly in establishing and strengthening your daily personal relationship with God is "Discovering God Through the Daily Practice of His Presence."[15] It explains in practical ways how one may cultivate God's presence each day.

THE TWO BIRTHS OF CHRIST

In order to understand what church membership is all about, we need to remember that there are not one but two births of Christ: one is His birth into the world when He was born in Bethlehem; the other is His birth in the soul when a person is spiritually reborn after baptism, lives in repentance, and receives Him regularly in the sacraments, especially the Eucharist.

It was on this second birth that St. Paul insisted when he wrote to the Ephesians, praying that Christ may dwell in their hearts by faith and that they may be rooted and grounded in love. This is the second Bethlehem, the daily personal relationship of the individual to the Lord Jesus, our Great Lover. This is what church membership means: the personal indwelling of Christ in the believer through the Eucharist and the daily practice of His presence. According to the Fathers, one of the main stages in our spiritual journey is direct personal union with God.

---

15   By Anthony M. Coniaris. Available through Light and Life Publishing Company, PO Box 26421, Minneapolis, MN 55426-0421.

I KNOW HIM

Being an Orthodox Christian is far more than being able to produce a baptismal certificate; it is the personal experience of the Risen Christ, living and reigning in our lives. It is inner peace and freedom, a new sense of direction and purpose in our lives. "I do not believe in God," someone said. "I know Him." "I know Him in whom I have believed," said St. Paul. "Having seen (experienced) the resurrection of Christ we worship the Lord Jesus," says one of the prayers of the Church. "It is one thing to believe in God, and another to know Him," said Staretz Silouan.

The following statement is from the previously mentioned report to Archbishop Iakovos on the "Future of Orthodoxy." Again, try to count how many times the word "personal" is used.

> *The overall answer to the cultural crisis of faith is a personal approach to the truths and values of the Orthodox faith. By personal is meant an internalization of these truths and values so that they may be held with a conscious personal conviction. To sustain the Orthodox identity we can no longer count on the spiritual investments of the past, that is to say, simply on the power of tradition and formal habits. We must also generate new spiritual investments ourselves in this secular but thirsting society by means of a spiritual rekindling of Orthodox souls with the grace of the love of Christ.*

BECOMING PRAYER

The purpose and goal of developing a daily, personal relationship with Jesus is expressed well by Fr. Goettmann, a French Orthodox priest in his book, "The Spiritual Wisdom and Practices of Early Christianity:"

> *We first "do" exercises, then we become exercise; we say prayers but we must eventually become prayer; we go to the liturgy but our whole being is called to become liturgical and daily life is meant to be a celebration; we seek to experience God, but in doing so, we ourselves become gods![16]*

DISCOVERING GOD IN THE PRESENT MOMENT

Since the Fathers teach that purity of heart is tantamount to being "single-minded" we must emphasize the need to make God central in our daily lives. By believing that God is actively involved in our daily lives, we can let go of our worries and anxieties about the future and live for God in the present moment, a moment filled with His presence and with the possibility of growing in His likeness. Thus we take no thought for tomorrow (Matt 6:24), knowing that each person we meet and each situation we are in can be an encounter with God. We need to learn to discover God in the present. Too often we are concerned with the future or lost in memories of the past; in doing so, we "miss" God in the present. This is why our daily, personal relationship with Christ is important. It helps us find God and His power in the present moment.

JESUS CALLS MARY BY NAME

At the end of John's gospel, we find Mary Magdalen outside the Lord's tomb. When the risen Christ appears to her, she is so near that she can touch Him, but she does not recognize Him, nor does she understand the meaning of what has happened. She is bewildered and depressed because she believes that now that her Lord is dead the foundations of her world have collapsed. But then the risen Jesus gets through to her with one word. He addresses her by name, "Mary." Upon hearing her name, she recognizes Jesus immediately, and replies personally and endearingly, "Raboni" which means "my Lord."

Jesus loves us personally and calls us by name. He says to Peter, "Peter, I have prayed for you that you may not fall..." If He prayed personally and by name for Peter, is He not doing the same for you and for me right now? Prayer in a sense is listening to Jesus as He prays for us by name? God's love is personal!

A foreign student from West Germany visited a young people's meeting at a church in the U.S. After he came home that evening he said to his friends, "They prayed for me by name. I have never heard my name said in prayer before." He was impressed because he had tasted the personal love of God for him. Yet should not we all taste this personal

---

16   "The Spiritual Wisdom and Practices of Early Christianity." Alphonce and Rachel Goettman. 1994. Inner Life Publishing. Greenwood, IN.

love? Does not God say to each one of us: "I have called you by name; you are mine" (Is 43:1).

A PICTURE WINDOW TO GOD'S HEART

Our personal love for others is but a reflection of His love for us. The 17th chapter of John's Gospel records what is known as the high priestly prayer which Jesus offered to His Father in the Upper Room at the Last Supper in the presence of His disciples. It is one of the most treasured chapters in all Scripture.

It shows us Jesus engaged in a wonderful kind of very personal praying. It is a very warm, intimate praying, a personal conversation, unhurried, relaxed, basking in the Father's presence. He talks with God heart-to-heart, praying for His disciples and all who through the centuries would come to believe in Him through their word. This beautiful high priestly prayer that Jesus began on earth does not end here. It continues in heaven where Jesus now intercedes for us constantly as our Advocate and Mediator before the throne of God the Father. How can any of us continue to live in discouragement if we truly believe that the risen and ascended Lord is praying for us?

Jesus is praying fervently and specifically for His disciples – those He would leave behind to continue His ministry. He includes us among the disciples when He prays in verse 20, "I do not pray for these only, but also for those who believe in me through their word..." We are the ones who today believe in Him through the word of the disciples. So, He is praying for us – for you and me.

JESUS PRAYS FOR YOU

We can read this chapter (John 17) in a very personal manner beginning with verse 6, inserting our name in place of the various pronouns:

> *I have manifested thy name to _____ whom thou*
> *gavest to me out of the world; _____ is thine,*
> *and thou gavest _____ to me; and _____ has kept*
> *thy word... I pray for _____: I pray not for the*
> *world, but for _____ whom thou hast given me,*
> *for _____ is thine... And now I am no more in the*
> *world, but _____ is in the world... I pray not that*

thou shouldest take _____ out of the world, but
that thou shouldest keep _____ from evil.

God loves us personally and prays for us personally and by name. Such personal prayer is very much in keeping with Luke's account of the Last Supper, where Jesus prays very personally for one of His disciples, Simon Peter: "Simon, Simon, behold Satan demanded to have you, that he might sift you like wheat, but I have prayed for you that your faith may not fail; and when you have turned again, strengthen your brethren" (Luke 22:31, 32).

MY GREETINGS TO PRISCA AND AQUILA

The warmth of the personal relationship that exists between God and us transforms our relationships to one another, making them more personal. St. Paul expresses this personal love in his warm greetings at the end of his letter to the Romans where he mentions and sends warm greetings to a host of persons by name and he takes sixteen verses to do so. At one time I considered these personal greetings superfluous. Only later did I discover that they reflect God's personal love for each one of us by name:

> *I commend to you our Sister Phoebe, the deaconess of the Church at Cenchreae. Give her, in union with the Lord, a welcome worthy of saints, and help her with anything she needs: she has looked after a great many people, myself included.*
>
> *My greetings to Prisca and Aquila, my fellow workers in Christ Jesus, who risked their lives for me. I am not the only one to owe them a debt of gratitude. So do all the Gentile Churches.*
>
> *Greetings also to the Church that meets at their house.*
>
> *Greetings to my dear Epaenetus, the first person in the province of Asia to give himself to Christ.*

48

Greetings to Mary who has worn herself out working for you.

Greetings to Andronicus and Junias, my kinsmen who were with me in prison, they are well known among the apostles and became Christians before I did.

Greetings to Ampliatus, dear to me in the Lord.

Greetings to Urban, our fellow worker in Christ and my beloved Stachys.

Greetings to Apelles who proved his devotion to Christ.

Greetings to everyone who belongs to the household of Aristobulus.

Greetings to Herodion, my kinsmen, and those of the household of Narcissus who belong to the Lord.

Greetings to Tryphaena and Tryphosa, who work hard in the service of the Lord; to my friend Persis who has done so much for the Lord; to Rufus, the chosen servant of the Lord, and to his mother who has also been a mother to me.

Greetings to Asyncritus, Phlegon, Hermes, Patrobas, Hermas, and all the brothers who are with them.

Greetings to Philologus and Julia, Nereus and his sister, and Olympas and all God's people who are with them.

Greet each other with a holy kiss. All the Churches of Christ send you greetings.

(Rom. 16, 1-16)

"I have called you by name. You are mine," says the Lord. God's love is personal.

When you finally appear before God, He will not say to you, "Well done, good and faithful servant;" He will speak to you very personally, by name, and say, "Well done, Nick, Mary, Jane, you have been faithful in little, I will set you over much. Come, inherit the kingdom prepared for you from the foundation of the world." When you hear your name called out by Jesus at the Second Coming that will be for you the beginning of heaven.

Chapter Six

Jesus:
Cosmic or Personal Savior?

No Russian Orthodox believer would think
to call this Jesus "personal." He is a cosmic
Savior – He does not belong to me alone.

– Fr. Anthony Ugolnik in
"The Illuminating Icon"

JESUS: COSMIC OR PERSONAL SAVIOR?

In his excellent book "The Illuminating Icon" Fr. Anthony Ugolnik writes,

> *Look to the ceiling of the worshiping churches in Russia and you will find a majestic icon of Jesus spread across the dome, looking down upon all gathered in His kingdom. Divine life comes to us in community. No Russian Orthodox believer would think to call this Jesus "personal." He is a cosmic Savior – He does not belong to me alone...*

> *Russian Christians, for example, are puzzled by the terminology that identifies Christ as "personal Savior." I have tried to explain that phrase to them, and they are somewhat baffled by the word "personal." "Like a wallet?" one of them asked with smile. "Or a toothbrush?" In their cosmology, Jesus is that divine agent by which all creation is related to divinity. Jesus is a Savior so great that He defies the personalist category.*[17]

A basic teaching of Orthodox theology is that Jesus is a Person. God the Father is a Person. God the Holy Spirit is a Person. The three Persons of the Holy Trinity do defy and supersede the "personalist category," but they are nonetheless three Persons in one essence!

To the person who says, "Jesus is not our personal but our cosmic Savior," the Church says, "He is both cosmic and personal. If salvation is to become real, the cosmic Savior must become our personal Savior. Salvation is personal but it is not private. We can be damned alone but we cannot be saved alone. We are saved in the Body of Christ, the Church, through a personal appropriation of our Lord's crucifixion and resurrection, which begins in baptism and continues through all of life.

---

17 "Illuminating Icon." A. Ugolnik. Wm. B. Eerdmans Co. 1989.

PANTOCRATOR AND BEST FRIEND

Jesus is indeed the Pantocrator, the all-powerful, all-ruling, cosmic, Lord of lords and King of kings, but He is at the same time a Person and our best Friend. We must let Him come down from that high dome to make His home in our hearts as our personal Savior and Friend. He is both transcendent and immanent. Though He cannot be "possessed" like a toothbrush, He desires greatly to dwell in us by grace. I have known great theologians and scientists who regard God with the deepest awe, yet at the same time know Him through Christ as a personal Friend and Savior. We need to remember that we did not first call Jesus "Friend." He took the initiative. He first called us friends. He initiates this personal relationship He wishes to have with us.

Daniel B. Clendenin clarifies what has often posed a problem for some in understanding the difference in emphasis in the Orthodox Church between the divine transcendence (incomprehensibility) and God's immanence and nearness to us. He writes,

> *Have the Eastern theologians stressed the divine transcendence to the point that they must deny His immanence, His nearness, His personal interaction with us? In fact, it seems that we have to answer in the affirmative. But if we left the Eastern fathers at this point we would do them a great disservice, for in addition to affirming the mystery of God, they equally insist on the necessity of mystical union with Him, and draw our attention to the many biblical statements about our knowing God in a personal way.* [18]

What is it about us Orthodox Christians that makes evangelical Christians say about us, "Orthodoxy? It's nearly all superstition. I pray that they will become born-again Christians. They need to know Jesus as their personal Savior." Are they speaking from ignorance or are they justified? How personal is my faith in Jesus? Do I try to make it personal to my children, my friends, my fellow parishioners?

18   "Eastern Orthodox Christianity." D.B. Clendenin. Baker Books. 1994.

UNITYING OUR THEOLOGIZING WITH A PERSONAL RELATIONSHIP

We do not merely learn about Jesus. We come to know Him personally. This is how we come to experience the living power of His presence in our lives. Sometimes some theologians are so preoccupied with talking about theology that they never experience the subject of their theologizing. We need to unite our theologizing with an everyday spirituality through a daily, personal relationship with Jesus. We need to proceed from theology to doxology. The Church Fathers say, "A theologian is one who truly prays. And one who truly prays is a theologian." A theologian is one who has a personal prayer relationship with God, lived out in the community of God's people, the Church.

We must not allow our evangelical Protestant friends to steal from us what has always been ours as Orthodox Christians, our daily personal relationship with Jesus as Lord and God.

BORN IN THE CHURCH

A personal relationship with Christ is essential but it does not grow on trees. It does not just happen somehow between you and Jesus. It is born in the Church. It is nourished in the Church. It grows in the Church. If this personal relationship with Jesus is not anchored in the Church, the Living Body of Christ, nourished by the true teachings of Jesus and the Sacraments, it will degenerate into a prideful egotism, a "Savior complex" that looks down on others as not saved. The Orthodox Church has always tried to maintain a balance between the faith of the individual and the faith of the Church, the community of God's people down through the ages. The two must never be separated.

Jesus said, "Anyone who loves me will keep my word and my Father will love him, and we shall come to him and make our home in him." Jesus states clearly that if we love God and keep His word, He will make His home in us.

If God has truly made His home in us, how can we not have a daily, personal relationship with Him through prayer, meditation, silence, the sacraments, and the reading of His word? How can we not enjoy and savor His presence each day?

Like the prodigal son who was embraced by his father, we need to kneel penitently each day before the Father to let Him embrace us; and as we kneel, to put our ears against His chest and listen, without interruption, to the heartbeat of His love. Eternal life begins now with a daily, personal relationship with Jesus.

A survey revealed that what most Americans want in their leaders is "a vague faith strongly held." What Jesus came to give us, however, is a deeply personal faith strongly held.

COLD-STORAGE RELIGION

Someone has come up with what he calls "cold-storage religion." In cold-storage religion you believe that God exists; you just don't worship Him. In cold-storage religion, you agree that Jesus died and rose from the dead; it's just that you don't follow Him. In cold-storage religion, you don't necessarily disagree with the Bible's teachings, it's just that you ignore them. In cold-storage religion, you may agree that marriage is the right context for sex, but you have a live-in lover anyway. You don't deny that all good things come from God; but you spend your money the way you want and give little or nothing to charity and the work of the Lord. In other words, your relationship with Christ is in cold-storage, like a corpse in a mortuary.

ST. SABA

Contrast this cold-storage religion with the following very personal meditation on the life of Christ written by St. John Saba, a spiritual elder and Syrian Father of the sixth century:

> *Carry Him in your bosom like Mary His mother.*
> *Come in with the Magi to offer Him your gifts.*
> *Take Him from Symeon so that you may also*
> *   carry Him upon your arms...*
> *When He changes water into wine be there to*
> *   fill the jars.*
> *Raise the stone from Lazarus in order to learn*
> *   what is the resurrection from the dead.*
> *Put your head with John upon His breast in*
> *   order to hear the beating of His heart which*
> *   pulsates with love for all the world...*
> *Take for yourself a morsel of the Bread which*
> *   He has broken during the Supper in order to*

unite with His Body and abide in Him forever...
Go out with Him to the Mount of Olives in
order to learn from Him worship and bending
of the knees, till your sweat falls down like His.
Stand up, my brother. Weary not but carry the
cross as it is time for departure. Stretch your
hands with Him for the nails...
Arise early while it is still dark. Go the the tomb
to see the marvelous resurrection.
Go with the others to a solitary place, and bow
to receive the last blessing before His
Ascension... Sit in the Upper Room to be
clothed with power from on high through the
divided tongues.

THE ONE WHOM JESUS LOVED

It seemed like a case of adding insult to injury the other day, when I received a letter addressed to "occupant" and marked "Personal and Confidential."

Is not this typical of today's impersonal machine age where we are addressed anonymously by computers and identified by a number. Not so with God's love. It is uniquely personal.

For example, the Apostle John writes about Jesus, "No one has ever seen God; the only Son, Who is in the bosom of the Father, He has made Him known" (John 1:18).

The very intimate, personal and loving relationship between God the Father and God the Son is captured by this beautiful expression: that Jesus lies "in the bosom of the Father."

At the Last Supper as the apostles were gathered around the table with Jesus, we read, "One of His disciples, whom Jesus loved, was lying close to the bosom of Jesus..." (John 13:23). That disciple "whom Jesus loved" was John. The intimate relationship of love that exists between the Father and the Son in the Holy Trinity is now replicated between God in the Person of Jesus and one of us, represented by the Apostle John (who lies on His bosom).

Jesus wants each of us to be in as close a relationship to Him as He is to the Father. As Jesus is "in the bosom of the Father," so God the Father wants us – you and me – to be "in the bosom of Jesus." It is to this kind of tender, loving, personal, intimate relationship with God that God invites us through prayer, through the Eucharist and through His word. The disciple "whom Jesus loves" is not only John or Lazarus but each one of us. This position "in the bosom of Jesus" is reserved not only for John but also for you and for me as we grow in our faith and love for Jesus. One cannot get more personal than to be in the bosom of Jesus. How does one get there? Through prayer! Through the Eucharist! Through repentance. Through a daily, personal relationship with Jesus.

"MY" JESUS

Fr. John Powell describes his own deeply personal relationship with Jesus as follows:

> *I should want you to know and love my Jesus,*
> *not me. At least, this is the way it should be. I*
> *say "my Jesus," although He really isn't my*
> *exclusive possession. I say "my Jesus," because*
> *He is the Jesus I know. He is the Jesus who is*
> *my best friend and constant companion. My*
> *whole day and life is a running conversation*
> *with this Jesus. If others could "bug my brain,"*
> *they would be astonished. "He is talking to*
> *someone all day who isn't really there." To*
> *which I would respond: "He is there only to the*
> *eyes and ears, to the mind and heart of faith. He*
> *said He would take up His abode in those who*
> *would believe in Him and love Him. And I do*
> *believe in Him and I do love Him." Would you*
> *believe that Jesus and I actually have*
> *"nicknames" for each other? Special names for*
> *special friends. It is this Jesus that I want to*
> *share with you. This is what the early*
> *Christians felt: "We want you to know our*
> *Jesus." So they wrote the story of His life, the*
> *Gospels, because they wanted us to know their*
> *Jesus. St. John begins his first Letter: "I want to*
> *tell you what my eyes have seen, what my ears*
> *have heard, and my hands have touched. I want*

you to know my Jesus." The Gospels themselves
were intended as a faith-portrait of Jesus. It was
indeed a portrait that was born of faith. The
only way to know Jesus is to believe in Him. We
can know Him only to the extent that we believe.
Of course, the Gospels are not objective history.
The evangelists couldn't write an objective
history about someone they loved so much. No
one could write an objective history of his or
her mother. Jesus was their life and their hope.
They wanted to share Him, not themselves, with
the whole world.[19]

However great the sacrifice we are making for Jesus, we are not doing it for anything so cold as duty or dogma or the dictates of a code: we are doing it for the best Friend we have. We are doing it for our Precious Lord and Savior Jesus. Anything we do for Him, any sacrifice, any burden, any price we have to pay is not really a sacrifice at all but life's greatest privilege.

DOCTRINES ARE WRAPPED UP IN A PERSON

When Lazarus died, Mary said to Jesus, "If you had been here... my brother would not have died." Jesus assured her that her brother will rise. Martha replied, "I know that he shall rise again at the last day." Martha believed in the doctrine of the resurrection. But Jesus immediately made it a personal thing: "I am the resurrection and the life" (Jn 11:24, 25). When we come to see that all of our so-called doctrines are wrapped up in a Person, then our theology becomes doxology! A continuous doxology such as that prayed constantly by the monks: "Doxa si o Theos..." "Glory to Thee, O Lord."

I conclude this chapter with the words of Daniel B. Clendenin:

God is not merely a transcendent object of
detached intellectual scrutiny. He is also an
immanent Subject who, as Gregory Palamas
and Simeon the New Theologian insisted, must
be experienced directly. Cyril of Jerusalem was

---

19   From a video program, "Jesus As I Know Him."

correct when he observed that God as the
object of intellectual study and God as the
Subject of a personal relationship cannot be
separated: "The method of godliness consists of
these two things: pious dogmas and the practice
of virtue. God does not accept dogmas apart
from good works. Nor does He accept words
that are not based on pious dogmas." For
Orthodoxy, true theology involves not only
intellectual erudition but a spiritual experience
with the living God; this conception can
correct Western models of theology which tend
to be academic reflection on propositions.[20]

---

20   "Eastern Orthodoxy: A Western Perspective." D.B. Clendenin. Baker Books. Grand Rapids, MI.
      1994.

Chapter Seven

Prayer is Personal

For there to be prayer there must be a specifically personal relationship with the living God. Evagrius calls it a "conversation."

PRAYER IS PERSONAL

What is prayer? It is nothing more than an ongoing love relationship with God the Father, the Son, and the Holy Spirit.

St. Theophan describes how personal prayer is when he writes, "The work of God is simple: It is prayer, children talking to their Father, without any subtleties." How do children talk to their parents? Abstractly? Impersonally? No! Very personally! "Daddy! Mommy!" Did not Jesus teach us to pray to our Father personally using the word "Abba," which means Daddy?

A CHRISTIAN PSYCHIATRIST TESTIFIES

Dr. Paul Tournier, a Swiss psychiatrist, tells how one of life's greatest discoveries came to him. He used to visit an old Christian pastor, who never let him go without praying with him. He was struck by the extreme simplicity of the old man's prayers. It seemed just a continuation of an intimate conversation that the old saint was always carrying on with Jesus. Paul Tournier goes on, "When I got back home I talked it over with my wife, and together we asked God to give us also the close fellowship with Jesus the old pastor had. Since then Jesus has been the center of my devotion and my traveling companion. He takes pleasure in what I do (cp. Eccl. 9:7), and concerns Himself with it. He is a friend with whom I can discuss everything that happens in my life. He shares my joy and my pain, my hopes and fears. He is there when a patient speaks to me from his heart, listening to him with me and better than I can. And when the patient is gone I can talk to Him about it." Therein lies the very essence of the Christian life.

FOLKSY CHATS WITH GOD

I have always enjoyed the scene in "Fiddler on the Roof" where Tevye says, "Dear God, You made many, many, many poor people. I realize that it's no shame to be poor, but it's no great honor either. So what would have been so terrible if I had a small fortune?" We delight in these fictional scenes where humans have folksy chats with God, but does not the psalmist do the same constantly as he converses with God?

THE JESUS PRAYER IS PERSONAL

What is our Orthodox practice of the Jesus Prayer but "an intimate intercourse of penitent sinners with the Reedemer," to quote Fr. George Florovsky. Praying the Jesus Prayer is part of our daily personal relationship with Jesus.

When a monk prays the Jesus Prayer in the Orthodox tradition, he drops his head to the chest or the heart to denote that, in praying, he is descending with his mind into his heart to make his prayer to Jesus personal. He enters the presence of God not just with his mind, but also with his heart. He is fully, completely and personally present to God.

Through the Jesus Prayer we come in contact with the Risen Christ. He is living and alive in our mind, in our heart, and in our breathing. Through this prayer "the heart swallows the Lord and the Lord the heart." Through the Jesus Prayer we enter into a personal relationship with God. Our spirit, soul, and body come to experience the God of peace and love in an intensely personal way as the heart, breathing rhythmically prays: "Lord Jesus, Son of God, have mercy on me, the sinner."

One of the saints of the Church said, "Heaven is God and God is in my heart." Through the Jesus Prayer God is, indeed, in the heart, and the heart becomes heaven. One of the great tragedies of our lives is that we do not experience that presence. Thus, our faith does not become truly real to us. Yet God wants us to experience His presence. This is why Christ came, why He suffered, died, and rose again; why He sent the Holy Spirit – to be always present to us in a truly personal and intimate way.

The Jesus Prayer is also referred to as "the prayer of the heart" because it rises from the deepest and most personal place of our being, from its very center, the heart.

INTIMATELY PERSONAL

To understand how intimately personal the Jesus Prayer is, focus on these words by Irma Zaleski:

> *Why, when we say the Jesus Prayer, do we say*
> *"have mercy on me, a sinner?" Why 'me' and*
> *not "us"? Should we not pray for mercy for*
> *everybody? Should we not pray for the whole*
> *Church? Of course. In a very real sense every*
> *prayer is a prayer of the Church. Apart from the*

*Church, the Body of Christ, our prayer means
nothing. We cannot pray the Jesus Prayer
outside the Church. When we say "Jesus" we
mean the whole Jesus, His whole body, the
whole of the redeemed universe. But, because it
is a prayer of repentance, the prayer of a sinner,
it must also be a prayer of each one alone. In
the final analysis, we have to make our own
individual peace with God, find our own
relationship with Him, meet Him face to face.
Nobody can do it for us.*[21]

And so we pray from the heart: "Lord Jesus, be merciful to me, the sinner."

THE AKATHISTOS HYMN TO THE SWEETEST JESUS

If you wish to see how truly personal and intimate prayer can be, I refer you to the Akathistos Hymn to the "Sweetest Jesus" as it is sung in the Orthodox Church. Listen to a few excerpts from that service:

*When the light of Thy truth shone in the world,
devilish delusion was driven away; for the
idols, O our Saviour, have fallen, unable to
endure Thy power. But we who have received
salvation cry to Thee:*

> *Jesus, Truth dispelling falsehood.*
> *Jesus, Light transcending every light.*
> *Jesus, King surpassing all in strength.*
> *Jesus, God constant in mercy.*
> *Jesus, Bread of life, fill me who am hungry.*
> *Jesus, Wellspring of knowledge, refresh me who
> am thirsty.*
> *Jesus, Garment of gladness, clothe me who am
> naked.*
> *Jesus, Haven of joy, shelter me who am
> unworthy.*

---

21   "Living the Jesus Prayer." I. Zaleski. White Horse Press. 1993.

Jesus, Giver to those who ask, grant me
 mourning for my sins.
Jesus, Finder of those who seek, find my soul.
Jesus, Opener to those who knock, open my
 hardened heart.
Jesus, Redeemer of sinners, wash away my sins.
Jesus, Son of God, have mercy on me.

When the blind man heard Thee, O Lord,
passing by on the way, he cried: Jesus, Son of
David, have mercy on me! And Thou didst call
him and open his eyes. Wherefore, by Thy mercy
enlighten the spiritual eyes of my heart as I cry
to Thee and say:

Jesus, Creator of those on high.
Jesus, Redeemer of those below.
Jesus, Vanquisher of the nethermost powers.
Jesus, Adorner of every creature.
Jesus, Comforter of my soul
Jesus, Enlightener of my mind.
Jesus, Gladness of my heart.
Jesus, Health of my body.
Jesus, my Saviour, save me.
Jesus, my Light, enlighten me.
Jesus, from all torment deliver me.
Jesus, save me who am unworthy.
Jesus, Son of God, have mercy on me.

O my Jesus Christ plenteous in mercy, accept
me who confess my sins, O Master, and save me,
O Jesus, and snatch me from corruption, O Jesus.

O sweetest Jesus, save us.

O my Jesus, no one else hath been so prodigal
as I, the wretched one, O Jesus Lover of mankind,
but do Thou Thyself save me, O Jesus.

O sweetest Jesus, save us.

THE PSALMIST

Prayer has to be personal. How can it be otherwise if it is a dialogue between two people who love each other. This is why the psalmist prays so personally:

> My soul clings to you (Ps 62:9).
>
> My soul thirsts for you (Ps 62:3).
>
> As a deer longs for the springs of water, so my soul longs for you, O God (Ps 121:1).
>
> I will love you, O God my strength (Ps 16:2).
>
> My soul is always in your hands (Ps 118:109).
>
> I will bless the Lord at all times; his praise will always be in my mouth (Ps 33:2).

TRUTH IS A PERSON

For Orthodox Christians truth is not an abstract idea. Truth is a Person. It is Christ. Christ Himself said, "I am truth" (Jn 13:16). And the Christ who is Truth is at the same time life as well. Thus, Christ is also the way in which we are called to live and walk daily in order to know the truth. Truth and Life are personal. "I am the Truth," said Jesus and "I am the Life." Ultimate truth is a Personal Being apprehended by love.

ST. SILOUAN

Archimandrite Sophrony writes about St. Silouan:

> "Christ's manifestation to Silouan was a personal encounter by virtue of which his approach to God acquired a deeply personal character. In prayer he conversed with God face to face. The feeling of God being Personal delivers prayer from the imagination and abstract argument, transporting everything into an invisible core of lively inward communion. Concentrated within, prayer ceases to be a 'cry into space', and the mind becomes all attention and listening. Calling upon the Divine Name –

*Father, Lord, and other appellations – Silouan
continued caught up in a state about which 'it is
not lawful for a man to speak'. But whoever has
himself experienced the presence of the living
God will understand."*[22]

COME UNTO ME

Someone wrote about Jesus,

*When he said to the weary, "Come unto me," I
know that the Savior was speaking to me. When
he prayed in the garden of Gethsemane, those
sweat drops of blood were flowing for me. When
the sword pierced his side and he felt agony,
when the nails ripped his hands, he suffered for
me. When he hung to his death on that cruel
tree, and cried, "Father, forgive them," he
pleaded for me. Though I can't comprehend it,
I'm certain that he, now sits beside God,
waiting for me!*

A wife writes about praying with her husband,

*During one difficult period in my life when I
was feeling much inner turmoil, my husband
would hold me close and simply ask God to be
with me that day. That brief ordinary ministry
was like an anointing to me. From time to time
we share a similar kind of morning prayer, as
we embrace each other while we pray.*

Holding one close as one prays – husband with wife, parent with
child – makes prayer so much more personal. It makes us feel embraced
by God's love.

Since prayer is so personal, we should never hesitate to come to God
spontaneously:

---

22   "St. Silouan the Athonite." Archimandrite Sophrony. Stavropegic Monastery of St. John the Baptist.
Essex, England. 1991.

When on the verge of losing our temper, to pray,
"Thy patience, Lord."
When alone, to pray, "Thy presence, Lord."
When anxious, to pray, "Thy peace, Lord."
When tempted by lustful thoughts, to pray, "Thy
purity, Lord."

Mother Teresa wrote about Pope John Paul II's personal relationship with God:

"Ever sustained by a profound faith, nourished
by unceasing prayer, fearless in unshakable
hope, deeply in love with God."

Sustained by profoundly personal prayer, we, too, will find ourselves deeply in love with God.

Our relationship to God can become so intimately personal that it will no longer need to be expressed through the use of words. Bishop Ware emphasizes this when he writes:

Praying, defined in this way, is no longer
merely to ask for things, and can indeed exist
without the employment of any words at all. It is
not so much a momentary activity as a
continuous state. To pray is to stand before
God, to enter into an immediate and personal
relationship with Him; it is to know at every
level of our being, from the instinctive to the
intellectual, from the sub- to the
supra-conscious, that we are in God and He is
in us. To affirm and deepen our personal
relationships with other human beings, it is not
necessary to be continually presenting requests
or using words; the better we come to know and
love one another, the less need there is to
express our mutual attitude verbally. It is the
same in our personal relationship with God.[23]

23   "The Power of the Name." Kallistos Ware. S.L.G. Press. Oxford, England. 1974.

SPEAK TO GOD HEART-TO-HEART

The very personal and intimate way in which Jesus p.~,~ ~~ Father inspired the great French preacher, Fenelon, to write these words, encouraging us to be just as intimate and personal in our prayers to Jesus:

> *Tell (God) all that is in your heart, as one*
> *unloads one's heart to a dear friend... Tell Him*
> *your troubles, that He may comfort you; tell*
> *Him your joys that He may sober them; tell Him*
> *your longings that He may purify them; tell Him*
> *your mislikings, that He may help you to*
> *conquer them; talk to Him of your temptations,*
> *that He may shield you from them; show Him*
> *all the wounds of your heart, that He may heal*
> *them. Lay bare to Him all your indifference to*
> *good, your depraved tastes for evil... your*
> *instability... If you thus pour out to Him all your*
> *weaknesses, needs and troubles, there will be no*
> *lack of what to say; you will never exhaust this*
> *subject, it is continually being renewed. People*
> *who have no secrets from each other never want*
> *subjects of conversation; they do not... weigh*
> *their words because there is nothing to be kept*
> *back. Neither do they seek for something to say;*
> *they talk together out of the abundance of their*
> *heart – without consideration, just what they*
> *think... Blessed are they who attain to such*
> *familiar, unreserved intercourse with God.*

OUR RESPONSE: INTIMACY

There can be no real relationship with Jesus the Bridegroom without this kind of a personal, loving intimacy. All life must be a deeper and deeper communion, an ever expanding Koinonia fellowship, between us and the Bridegroom Jesus. St. Ephrem speaks of the body and heart as the bridal chamber for Christ the Bridegroom. Our love for Him must be consummated daily in prayer, in His word, and the sacraments, especially the Eucharist through which we truly become one with Him. The Eucharist is indeed the celebrated marriage by which the most Holy Bridegroom espouses the Church as His Bride. It is by this mystery that we become "Flesh of His flesh, and bone of His bones" (Genesis 2:21).

An ingenious teenager, tired of reading bedtime stories to his little sister, decided to record several of her favorite stories on tape. He told her, "Now you can hear your stories anytime you want. Isn't that great?"

She looked at the machine for a moment and then replied, "No. It hasn't got a lap."

We all need a lap. We all need the closeness of relationship. We all need to know we are loved deeply and personally. A daily, personal relationship with Jesus enables us to sit on His lap each day.

THE ALTAR OF THE HEART

The Church Fathers have always considered the heart as the real place of prayer. Sebastian Brock writes:

> *One of the aspects of the heart is its interior liturgical role: it is the altar inside the sanctuary of the temple constituted by the body (1 Cor. 6:19), and on this altar the interior offering of prayer should continuously be made. Such an idea of prayer as an offering was already familiar from the Old Testament (e.g. Ps 141:2), while in the Syriac Bible (Sir 39:5) it is specifically stated that the heart is where prayer should take place. In the passages from Aphrahat and Ephrem we find that the location where the offering of prayer should be made is likewise identified as the heart, on the basis of Matthew 6:6, "Pray to your Father in secret, with the door shut," following an exegesis of the passage also found in Origen and Ambrose. In the Book of Steps the "altar of the heart" features prominently: in this work we have the concept of a three-dimensional liturgy which should take place simultaneously in the visible church on earth, in the church of the heart of the individual Christian, and in the heavenly church.*[24]

St. Nicodemos the Hagiorite calls the heart a shelter: "St. Isaac called the heart, 'the house of understanding.' As the animals when troubled and frightened run to their dens to be protected, so the mind of man, when troubled, runs to the heart and shouts, 'My Jesus help me! My Jesus save me!' and is thus liberated."[25]

ENTERING THE ALTAR OF THE HEART

St. Syngletike urges us to cense the altar of the heart "with the divine incense of prayer. For as poisonous creatures are sent away by certain strong poisons, so are evil thoughts banished by prayer..."

John Cassian urges us to enter the inner sanctuary, the "altar of the heart" often. He suggests frequent short prayers which because of their intensity avoid distraction. He writes,

> *We are praying in our inner room when we*
> *withdraw our heart completely from the*
> *clamour of our thoughts and preoccupations,*
> *and in a kind of secret dialogue, as between*
> *intimate friends, we lay bare our desires before*
> *the Lord.*

St. John Chrysostom reminds us that for prayer to be truly personal, it must come not just from the mouth but from the heart:

> *By prayer I mean not that which is only in the*
> *mouth, but that which springs up from the*
> *bottom of the heart. In fact, just as trees with*
> *deep roots are not shattered or uprooted by*
> *storms... in the same way prayers that come*
> *from the bottom of the heart, having their roots*
> *there, rise to heaven with complete assurance*
> *and are not knocked off course by the assault of*
> *any thought. That is why the psalm says: "Out*
> *of the deep I called unto thee, O Lord" (Psalm*
> *120:1).*

24   "The Syriac Fathers on Prayer and the Spiritual Life." Sebastian Brock. Cistercian Publ. 1987.
25   "Nicodemos of the Holy Mountain." Translated by Peter A. Chamberas. Paulist Press. 1989.

St. Theophan the Recluse explains that God responds to a truly personal prayer with "a certain feeling of warmth,"

When you establish yourself in the inner man by the remembrance of God, then Christ the Lord will enter and dwell within you. The two things go together.

And here is a sign for you, by which you can be certain that this glorious work has begun within you: you will experience a certain feeling of warmth towards the Lord. If you fulfill everything prescribed, then this feeling will soon begin to appear more and more often, and in time will become continuous. This feeling is sweet and beatific, and from its first appearance it stimulates us to desire and seek it, lest it leave the heart: for in it is Paradise.

Someone said, "The call of the God of the desert is precisely the call of prayer, that one-on-one dialogue with God, monos pros monon."

Chapter Eight

The Sacraments are Personal

Each one of us is the person for whom Christ shed that particular drop of blood.

– Blaise Pascal

THE SACRAMENTS ARE PERSONAL

The sacraments are not the "machines of salvation," or magical contacts that work automatically; they are rather personal encounters with Christ in faith.

Fr. George Florovsky writes:

> The climax of the Sacrament (Eucharist) is in
> the Presence of Christ... and in the personal
> encounter of the faithful with their Living Lord,
> as participants at His "Mystical Supper." The
> utter reality of this encounter is vigorously
> stressed in the office of preparation for
> Communion, as also in the prayers of
> Thanksgiving after Communion. The
> preparation is precisely for one's meeting with
> Christ in the Sacrament, personal and
> intimate... personal emphasis in all these
> prayers is dominant and prevailing. This
> personal encounter of believers with Christ is
> the very core of Orthodox devotional life.[26]

The personal aspect of the sacraments as an encounter between the believer and Christ is expressed in the manner by which the Eucharist is administered in the Orthodox Church. It is always personal. The name of each communicant is mentioned by the priest as one receives the Eucharist.

Repeating the words of our Lord, the priest says, "Take, eat...for you my body is broken...Drink of it all of you, for you was my blood shed..." For you the broken Body! For you the shed blood! For the forgiveness of your sins and for your everlasting life. The invitation our Lord directs to us for the Eucharist is clearly personal.

THE CHAPEL OF ADAM

There is a beautiful tradition which states that Adam was buried at the exact site on Golgotha where Jesus was crucified, and there Adam was the first to be baptized in the water and blood that flowed from the

---

26   "Aspects of Church History." G. Florovsky. Nordland Publ. Co. Belmont, MA.

side of Jesus on the cross (John 19:34). Many icons of the crucified Jesus show the water and blood flowing from Jesus' body onto the skull of Adam which is depicted at the foot of the cross. Thus, the first to sin is the first to be cleansed and clothed with the robe of God's righteousness. That is the reason the Greek Orthodox Church to this day maintains a chapel in Jerusalem over the exact site where Jesus was crucified and calls that chapel: The Chapel of Adam. To get to it one climbs a series of steep stone steps in the Church of the Holy Resurrection and suddenly finds oneself at Golgotha with a hole in the rock where the cross of Jesus was anchored.

When I see this beautiful icon of the crucifixion with the skull of Adam at the base of the cross, I try always to see myself in that skull of Adam. I prostrate myself before the Crucified Christ and I pray, "Lord, let the water and the blood from your side flow upon me constantly – the water: to wash me of my sins, in baptism as in tears of repentance that I shed daily for my sins; the blood: shed for me and so graciously offered in the Eucharist, to bring your Presence to me daily 'for the forgiveness of sins and unto life everlasting.'" It is only as we try to place ourselves in the icon of the crucifixion that it begins to have meaning for us. For, it was for me that He died; for me that He hung on the cross. Blaise Pascal wrote, "Each one of us is the person for whom Christ shed that particular drop of blood."

Bishop Ware writes, "The sacraments are personal. They are means whereby God's grace is appropriated to every Christian individually"[27]

THE EUCHARIST IS PERSONAL

Not until we say "Yes" to a person are we actually married. We said "Yes" to Jesus in baptism. This love is continually consummated in the Eucharist through which we not only cleave to the Body of Christ, but intermingle with it. We become not merely one body with Him, but one spirit. St. Gregory Palamas wrote:

> *O many-sided and ineffable communion! Christ*
> *has become our brother, for He has fellowship*
> *with us in flesh and blood... He has made us His*
> *friends, bestowing on us by grace these His*

---

27   "The Orthodox Church." T. Ware. Penquin Books. Baltimore, MD. 1963.

*sacraments. He has bound us to Himself and
united us, as the bridegroom unites the bride to
himself, through the communion of this His
blood, becoming one flesh with us. He has also
become our father through divine baptism in
Himself, and He feeds us at His own breast, as
a loving mother feeds her child.*

The Eucharist is our personal presence at the Last Supper. It is our personal encounter with the living Christ. This is where we meet Him and invite Him into our soul. Every time we partake of the Eucharist, we eat of the tree of life (Matthew the Poor).

Through the Eucharist we are present personally at the Last Supper. The same Master is present. The same bread. The same cup. The same sacrifice. The same Upper Room. The same Holy Spirit. The same Pentecost.

When we receive the Body and Blood of Jesus, we hear our name mentioned, "The servant of God _____ receives the precious Body and Blood of our Lord and Savior Jesus Christ for the forgiveness of sins and unto life everlasting." It is a joy for us to hear our name each time we receive the Eucharist. It is an assurance that God knows us by name and that He loves us in a very personal way which each one of us can hear and understand. Moreover, the prayers of the Eucharist are all very personal, i.e., "May the communion of Your holy mysteries be neither to my judgment nor to my condemnation, O Lord, but to the healing of soul and body." "I believe, O Lord, and confess that you are truly the Son of God..."

A CLOSE, LINGERING, LASTING RELATIONSHIP

"A man once gave a great banquet, and invited many, and at the time for the banquet he sent his servant to say to those who had been invited, 'Come for all is now ready.'"

Why come? Come because the banquet is now ready! The Greek word used for "banquet" here is deipnon. The word is significant in that it tells us about the kind of relationship Jesus wishes to establish with us once we come to Him. The early Greeks had three meals a day. Breakfast, akratisma, was not more than a piece of dried bread dipped into wine. The midday meal, called ariston, was simply a picnic snack eaten by the side of the road, or under a tree. The evening meal, deipnon, was the main

76

meal of the day. People lingered long at this meal, for the day's work was done and they were unhurried, with much to talk about. Thus the fact that in the Eucharist Jesus invites us to a deipnon, a banquet, describes the close, lingering, lasting, personal, and intimate relationship that He wishes to establish with each one of us.

The invitation to a meal is an invitation to intimacy with Jesus. This is especially true with the Last Supper where as we come, we pray personally:

> *Of Thy Mystic Supper, O Son of God, receive me today as a communicant; for I will not speak of the Mystery to Thine enemies; nor will I give Thee a kiss as did Judas; but like the thief do I confess Thee: Remember me, O Lord, in Thy Kingdom.*

> *Into the splendour of Thy Saints how shall I, the unworthy one, enter? For should I dare to enter the bridechamber, my vesture doth betray me, for it is not a wedding garment; and as one bound, I shall be cast out by the Angels. Cleanse, O Lord, the defilement of my soul, and save me, since Thou art the Friend of man.*

> *I am not sufficient, O Master and Lord, that Thou shouldest enter under the roof of my soul; but since Thou, as the Friend of man, dost will to dwell in me, with trust I draw nigh. Thou commandest; I will open wide the gates which Thou alone hast fashioned, that Thou mayest enter, in Thy wonted love for man, that Thou mayest enter and enlighten my darkened thought.*

> *May Thy holy Body, O Lord Jesus Christ our God, be unto me for eternal life, and Thy precious Blood for the forgiveness of sins. And may this Eucharist be unto me for joy, health, and gladness. And in Thy dread second coming, make me, the sinner, worthy to stand at the right hand of Thy glory, by the intercessions of Thine all-immaculate Mother and of all Thy Saints.*

> *Amen.*

BAPTISM IS PERSONAL

Just as the Eucharist is our personal presence at the Last Supper, so Baptism is our personal Golgotha and our personal resurrection or Pascha. We plunge into the waters of baptism as if we were plunging into death, and we come out of them to newness of life. We die with Christ and we rise with Christ. His death becomes our death; His resurrection becomes our resurrection.

The fact that baptism is our personal resurrection is expressed in the prayers of the Church. After the reading of the morning resurrection Gospel on Sundays, the congregation prays, "We have seen the resurrection of Christ..." Saint Symeon the New Theologian observes that the prayer does not say, "We have *believed* the resurrection of Christ...," but, "We have *seen* the resurrection of Christ... that is, the resurrection of Christ occurs in each of the faithful." Thus, beginning with baptism we experience personally the resurrection of Christ as He raises us by grace through repentance to newness of life. Daily we die with Him to sin; daily we rise with Him to newness of life.

At baptism we were personally betrothed to Christ the Bridegroom. We entered into a marriage relationship with Him that requires love and faithfulness. Our challenge as Orthodox Christians is to make a conscious, personal, deliberate confession of faith in the Person of Jesus and to keep renewing this confession in every liturgy as we confess our baptismal faith through the Nicene Creed. Thus, holiness is personal and relational. It is having a daily, personal relationship with Jesus through prayer, His word and the sacraments.

At baptism I was given a name and I entered into a personal relationship with Christ. He knows me by name. He says, "I know my own and My own know Me, as the Father knows me and I know the Father."

PRAYER MAKES BAPTISMAL GRACE PERSONAL

Commenting on the relation that exists between prayer and Baptism, St. Gregory of Sinai wrote, "Prayer is the manifestation of Baptism." Commenting on this statement Bishop Ware indicates that "For the overwhelming majority... Baptism is something received in infancy, of which we have no conscious memory. Although the baptismal Christ and the indwelling Paraclete never cease for one moment to work within

78

us, most of us – save on rare occasions – remain virtually unaware of this inner presence and activity. The prayer, then, signifies the rediscovery and manifestation of baptismal grace. To pray is to pass from the state where grace is present in our hearts secretly and unconsciously, to the point of full inner perception and conscious awareness when we experience and feel the activity of the Spirit directly and immediately. In the words of St. Kallistos and St. Ignatios (14th century), 'The aim of the Christian life is to return to the perfect grace of the Holy and Life-Giving Spirit, which was conferred on us at the beginning in divine Baptism.'"[28]

According to this statement, the Presence of Jesus and the grace conferred upon us in Baptism, become manifest and conscious in us when we pray. They erupt within us to make the presence of God active and real in our lives. Thus, the more we pray, the more we begin to feel and experience the baptismal presence of God in a personal way.

A PERSONAL RESPONSE IS REQUIRED

Just as God's love for each one of us is personal, so must our love for Him be personal. For this reason Baptism demands a personal response on the part of the baptized child when he/she grows to adulthood. The child must accept what God did for him or her in baptism. For baptism is not a divine pass that will get us into heaven automatically. Dr. Nikos Nissiotis has said, "A baptized Christian – especially in the Churches in which infant baptism is practiced – needs to make a personal decision regarding the Christian faith which he has passively inherited from his Christian environment."

Fr. Theodore Stylianopoulos has written,

> *As the baptized Christian grows from child to*
> *adult, and participates in the sacramental life of*
> *the Church, his personal response to God*
> *becomes crucial. Each Christian must*
> *personally re-affirm the baptismal pledge and*
> *himself say by free choice to Christ: Yes, I am*
> *yours! Spiritual renewal comes from this adult*
> *commitment to Christ, sharing in the Eucharist,*

---

28   "The Power of the Name." Bishop Kallistos of Diokleia. S.L.G. Press. Fairacres Oxford. 1974.

> *daily prayer, and sincere efforts to live the kind*
> *of life Christ lived and preached.*

Diadochus of Photike wrote,

> *When people are baptized, grace hides her*
> *presence until the soul makes a decision. When*
> *the whole person has turned to the Lord, then*
> *with an unspeakable tenderness grace reveals*
> *her presence to the heart.*

Fr. John Meyendorff wrote about the importance of the personal commitment that must take place in a Christian's life following baptism:

> *We are told in the Gospels that religious*
> *education implies a positive acceptance of*
> *Christ. This is the real conversion. If this*
> *marriage does not take place at some time*
> *during the life of a Christian, he is simply not a*
> *Christian. We have a very clear statement about*
> *this in the tradition of the Fathers. What makes*
> *a Christian a Christian is this personal*
> *commitment to Christ. One's formal belonging*
> *to the church through baptism and other*
> *sacramental participation remains a mere*
> *potential if the individual commitment does not*
> *take place. The sacramental gifts of Baptism*
> *and Eucharist and of all the sacraments are*
> *essential for an objective membership in the*
> *body of Christ; but again they are pure*
> *potentials if they are not taken seriously and if a*
> *conversion of the heart and mind does not*
> *occur at some point in one's life.*

CHRISMATION: OUR PERSONAL PENTECOST

Just as baptism is our personal Golgotha and our personal Pascha, so Chrismation is our personal Pentecost. Bishop Ware writes,

> *What happened to the first Christians on the*
> *day of Pentecost happens also to each of us*
> *when, immediately following our Baptism, we*

are in the Orthodox practice anointed with
Chrism or myron... The newly-baptized, whether
infant or adult, is marked (sealed cross-wise) by
the priest on the forehead, eyes, nostrils, mouth,
ears, breast, hands and feet, with the words,
"The seal of the gift of the Holy Spirit." This is
for each one a personal Pentecost: the Spirit,
who descended visibly upon the Apostles in
tongues of fire, descends upon every one of us
invisibly, yet with no less reality and power.
Each becomes an "anointed one," a "Christ"
after the likeness of Jesus... From the moment of
our Baptism and Chrismation, the Holy Spirit,
together with Christ, comes to dwell in the
innermost shrine of our heart. Although we say
to the Spirit, "Come," he is already within us.[29]

If we pray the hours for each day, then every day at 9 am (which is when Pentecost occurred) we invite the same Holy Spirit to come and dwell in us.

We know that our relationship with God is one that will endure for all eternity. It will not come to an end as all other relationships will. It is for this reason that it should be a deeply personal and living relationship with the One who "loved me and gave Himself for me."

PRAYING THE HOURS

Another way to enhance our daily personal relationship with God is by praying the hours each day. The Church planted prayer into each day by breaking the day into the following hours of prayer:

The first hour, 7 a.m. The dawning sun reminds us of Jesus who is the light of the world. We pray for guidance through the day:

Lord, Lord,
both day and night belong to You,
You formed the light and the sun
and marked the bounds of the earth.

---

29   "The Orthodox Way." K. Ware. SVS Press. Crestwood, NY. 1979.

And so we pray:
let Your great mercy
shine on our wretchedness
like the dawning light;
free us from the darkness
and from the shadow of death,
and from all the attacks and snares
of the evil one.

VERSE: *This is the day that the Lord has made,*
let us rejoice and be glad in it.

The third hour, 9 a.m. The hour of Pentecost. We thank God for sending the Holy Spirit on Pentecost and we pray for the Spirit's presence with us throughout the day:

O Lord, who didst send down Thy Most Holy
Spirit upon Thine Apostles at the third hour,
take Him not from us, O good One, but renew
Him in us.

VERSE: *Create in me a clean heart, O God, and*
put a new and right spirit within me. Cast me
not away from Thy presence, and take not Thy
Holy Spirit from me.

The sixth hour, noon. We pause at that, the moment of His crucifixion, to thank Him for His great love for us:

O Lord, who at the sixth hour was crucified for
our sake, forgive us, through Thy great love for
us.

VERSE: *Before Thy cross we bow down in*
worship, O Master, and Thy Holy resurrection
we glorify.

The ninth hour, 3 p.m. We remember Him Who expired in our behalf at that very hour:

O Lord, who at the ninth hour didst destroy the
power of death by Thy death, make us worthy to
share in Thy victory and life eternal.

VERSE: *I shall take the cup of salvation and call upon the name of the Lord. The Lord is my Light and my Salvation, of whom then shall I be afraid.*

The twelfth hour, 6 p.m. As the sun sets and darkness comes upon us, we remember that Jesus came to be "a light for revelation to the Gentiles." We pray:

Vouchsafe, O Lord, to keep us this night without sin. Blessed art Thou, O Lord, the God of our fathers, and praised and glorified be Thy name forever.

> **VERSE:** *Lord, now lettest Thou Thy servant depart in peace, according to Thy Word; for my eyes have seen Thy salvation.*

Compline, 9 p.m. Consists of prayers offered after supper:

Remember, O Lord, Thy departed servants (NAMES). Grant them rest where there is neither sickness nor sorrow nor sighing, but life everlasting.

> **VERSE:** *Our help comes from the Lord who made heaven and earth.*

Before retiring for the night.

Into Thy hands, I commend my spirit.

> **VERSE:** *Grant that I may behold Thy Kingdom all the days of my life.*

A good book to use for praying the hours is, "A Manual of the Hours of the Orthodox Church," which has the prayers for each hour in abbreviated form. An excellent book to use to help your children establish their own daily personal relationship with God is "Making God Real in the Orthodox Christian Home." It is filled with practical suggestions on how to involve children in prayer and church life.[30]

---

30   Both books are available through Light and Life Publishing Company.

Chapter Nine

The Personal Aspect of Faith and Prayer as Expressed in Orthodox Worship and Spirituality

I bring tears, purely, O Savior, from my eyes
and groans from the depths, crying aloud from
my heart: O God, I have sinned against Thee,
be merciful to me.
                    – The Canon of St. Andrew

THE PERSONAL ASPECT OF FAITH AND PRAYER AS EXPRESSED IN ORTHODOX WORSHIP AND SPIRITUALITY

Speaking on how personal God's promises are, Fr. Alexander Schmemann wrote,

> *Faith surely is this: the mysterious certitude that what Christ did and said, He did for me, He told me; that neither time nor space can separate Him from me, that nothing separates Him from me except my little faith, my forgetfulness, my innumerable betrayals.*[31]

I share with you this very personal prayer written by a Monk of the Eastern Church:

> *O Lord Jesus Christ our God, as you wept over Lazarus and shed tears of sadness and compassion for him, accept these bitter tears of mine.*
>
> *By your passion heal my passions, by your wounds comfort my wounds, by your blood purify my blood, and spread over my body the life-giving perfume of your body.*
>
> *The gall which your enemies offered you brings sweetness to my soul and makes it lose the bitterness which the enemy poured upon it.*
>
> *May your body stretched on the wood of the cross make my mind fly toward you when the demon tries to drag it down below.*
>
> *May your head which had to rest on the cross lift up my head when I am insulted by enemies.*
>
> *May your sacred hands nailed to the cross by unbelievers draw me up toward you from the abyss of perdition, as you yourself have promised (Jn. 12:32).*

---

31   "Celebrations of Faith,. Vol. 1." A. Schmemann. SVS Press. Crestwood, NY. 1991. page 17.

May your face which was so often struck by the slaps and spittle of cruel men make my face shine again after it has been disfigured by sin.

May your spirit which you gave back to your Father on the cross lead me to you by your grace.

I am without a heart that mourns and looks for you; I lack the spirit of penance and compunction that brings children back to their heritage.

I cannot weep, O Lord. My mind is clouded with earthly concerns and cannot direct its attention in sorrow.

My heart has grown cold from a multitude of temptations and can no longer warm itself with tears of love for you.

But may you, Lord Jesus Christ, treasury of blessings, grant me perfect repentance and a sorrowful heart that I may set myself to follow you with all my strength.

Without you I can do nothing good. Give me your grace, O generous one! May the Father who from all eternity engendered you from his bosom renew in me the features of your image and likeness.

A prayer as personal as the above is not unusual. It springs from the heart of one who has a deeply personal relationship with the Lord. Did not Jesus promise: "Rivers of living water shall flow from the belly of him who believes in me" (John 7:38).

THE CANON OF ST. ANDREW

Another example of how personal Orthodox prayers and worship services are is the Canon of St. Andrew. Study some of the hymns from this service and see how much the personal prevails:

There is no sin in life, no deed, no wickedness, which I, O Saviour, have not committed, in mind and in word, of intent, of design, and of thought, and in deed I have sinned as none ever has done.

In night I have ever passed my life: for the night of sin has been for me darkness and deep mist: but show me, O Saviour, to be as a son of day.

I bring tears, purely, O Saviour, from my eyes, and groans from the depths, crying aloud from my heart: O God, I have sinned against thee, be merciful to me.

My soul, my soul, arise, why sleepest thou? The end draws near, and thou shalt be confounded: therefore rise up, that Christ God may spare thee, he who is everywhere, and filleth all things.

We have sinned, we have trespassed, we have dealt unrighteously before thee, we have not observed, nor have we done, according to thy commandment. But deliver us not to the end, God of our Fathers.

Christ became man, calling to repentance thieves and harlots: O soul, repent, the door of the Kingdom is already opened: Pharisees and Publicans seize it before thee, and adulterers repenting.

I am clothed in the raiment of shame, like the leaves of the fig tree, for reproach of my self-willed passions.

I wear a coat of disgrace, and shamefully stained with blood, the flow of a life of passion, and of lust.

I have sunk beneath the weight of passions, and the corruption of material things: and hence the enemy now assails me.

Lover of material things, I preferred, O Saviour, a life in love with possessions to one unpossessed, and now I am hung about with a burdensome collar.

I adorned the image of the flesh, with shameful thoughts, the cloak of many colours, and I am condemned.

I assiduously sought to adorn the outside alone, despising the inner tabernacle, in the pattern of God.

I have discoloured the pristine image of beauty, O Saviour, with passions: but, as once the drachma, seeking, find it.

I have sinned, as the Harlot, I cry unto thee, alone I have sinned against thee: even so, O Saviour, accept, as myrrh, my tears.

Be merciful, as the Publican, I cry unto thee, O Saviour, be merciful to me: for there is none out of Adam, who has sinned, as I have, against thee.

PERSONAL PARTICIPATION IN THE LITURGY

Another way by which we may deepen our faith and make it more real is by participating personally in the liturgy. We are not mere spectators in the liturgy. The liturgy itself calls for our very personal participation.

Fr. Stanley Harakas highlights the importance of our participation in the Liturgy when he writes,

The text of the liturgy... invites the participation of the worshipper in concrete and specific fashion. No, one could even say that the text of the Liturgy, begs, requires, yes, demands participation... without that participation a large portion of its riches remain closed to us.[32]

---

32   "The Melody of Prayer." S. Harakas. Light and Life Publishing Company. Minneapolis, MN. 1979. page 15.

Fr. Stanley proceeds to mention at least ten specific ways of participating personally in the Liturgy. One of the most important ways, of course, is by receiving the precious Body and Blood of Jesus in the Holy Eucharist. This is, indeed, a very personal encounter between Christ and the communicant as is indicated in the pre-Communion prayers.

Fr. Stanley proceeds to point out that the litanies of the Liturgy are addressed by the priest not to God but to the worshippers:

> *The priest or deacon is addressing himself to the congregation. The Liturgy is thus directing the believer to pray, while at the same time providing the content of the prayer: peace for the world, ecclesiastical stability, and the unity of all believers, etc. The singing of "Kyrie Eleison" may be perceived as signifying assent, but precisely speaking it is not a response to the liturgical directive to pray for peace, stability and union. The only appropriate response for the participating worshipper is to, in fact, offer a prayer of his or her own words in which all or some of these become subjects of a personally uttered prayer. One way would be to simply rephrase the petition, directing it as a prayer to God: "O Lord, grant peace to the whole world, as well as stability and unity for your Church." This could be done quietly and quickly as well, so that the worshipper could join in with the "Kyrie Eleison."* [33]

When praying for "the sick and the suffering" we can quickly pray by name for those among the sick and suffering whom we know. When praying for "peace in the world," we can pray for those who are estranged and need to be reconciled, etc. If the priest is directing us to pray for peace, for the sick and the suffering, etc., and we do not respond to these biddings, then nobody is praying. Our personal participation is crucial.

Other ways of personal participation in the Liturgy are: singing the hymns of the Liturgy, listening attentively to the readings of Scripture,

---

33   Op Cit p 26.

making the sign of the cross, praying the Lord's Prayer, the Creed, the pre-Communion prayers, etc. The Liturgy comes alive when we respond to its call for us to participate in it personally.

THE DAILY RULE OF PRAYER

The Church has given us what is known as the Daily Rule of Prayer to help us develop and deepen our daily personal relationship with God.

The wisdom behind the daily rule of prayer is that one has to set aside a regular period of time each day and devote it exclusively to prayer, to uniting oneself to God. In other words, "You cannot wait to be in the mood of prayer; you have to use the spur of your Prayer Rule to force yourself to pray," as Sergei Fudel writes in his excellent book "Light in the Darkness."[34]

Our Orthodox tradition also provides a basic outline of content for the Daily Rule of Prayer which begins with a simple invocation of the name of God, i.e., we make the sign of the cross and say, "In the Name of the Father and of the Son and of the Holy Spirit. Amen." This is followed by the prayer to the Holy Spirit, "O Heavenly King...." This is followed in turn by the Trisagion Prayers. Of course, this is only the beginning of the Rule of Prayer. It may go on and include the reading of a psalm, a Scripture reading, the Nicene Creed, some of the petitions from the liturgy, a period of silence, special petitions of praise and thanksgiving, intercessions for other people, extemporaneous prayers, devotional readings, etc. It can be as long or as short as one desires.

THE DAILY HOURS OF PRAYER

The rule of prayer may be used for morning or evening prayers, or for both. Your spiritual Father can assist you in establishing such a rule of prayer. An Orthodox prayer book can also be very helpful. A daily devotional book such as "Daily Vitamins for Spiritual Growth"[35] can be of benefit.

The great advantage of using a rule of prayer is that it never lets a day go by without a personal conversation with God. Soon prayer becomes a habit that enriches each day and goes beyond just throwing up a prayer in daily emergencies. Such discipline makes our relationship with God deeply

---

34 SVS Press. Scarsdale, N.Y.
35 Available through Light and Life Publishing Company. PO Box 26421, Minneapolis, MN. 55426-0421.

personal and bears spiritual fruit. "All discipline for the moment seems not to be joyful, but sorrowful; yet to those who have been trained by it, afterwards it yields the peaceful fruit of righteousness" (Hebrews 12:11).

St. Symeon the New Theologian tells of a young man in Constantinople who, as he was practicing his rule of prayer one day, was surrounded by a divine radiance. He forgot the whole world and became one with the light of Christ. When the vision vanished, he was full of joy and wonder, his eyes shedding tears of joy and his heart filled with great sweetness. St. Symeon related this experience to show that it is possible to live in the world and still achieve the essence of Christian life – a personal knowledge and relationship with the living Christ.

Fr. Chas. Bell writes,

> *One of the advantages I have found in using a rule of prayer is that it takes away the burden of needing to be creatively new each time I pray. On many occasions I do not feel creative or particularly inspired. At such times, through the rule of prayer, I am able to enter into the joy and depth of using prayers that were inspired by the Holy Spirit and have been used by Christians for centuries.*
>
> *I have started out with the intention to pray on a daily basis many times, but usually can only maintain the practice so long as I feel inspired. When I no longer feel the inspiration that led me to the discipline in the first place, I gradually stop the practice.*
>
> *However, by using a rule of prayer I have found it possible to continue a daily discipline of prayer even when I don't feel like it. On those occasions when I don't feel spiritual, and consequently am unable to be spontaneous in prayer, the rule allows me to pray anyway and covers all of the areas I would want to cover. Over time, this daily spiritual discipline bears fruit.*[36]

36   "Discovering the Rich Heritage of Orthodoxy." C. Bell, PhD. Light and Life Publishing Company. 1994

Chapter Ten

The Personal Aspect of the Creed, the Trinity, Theology and Sacred Tradition

Tradition is the living faith of the dead;
traditionalism is the dead faith of the living.

– Jaroslav Pelikan

THE PERSONAL ASPECT OF THE CREED, THE TRINITY, THEOLOGY, AND SACRED TRADITION

The Nicene Creed – the Symbol of our Faith – adopted by the whole Church as the official Confession of our Orthodox Faith, is in the first person singular, "I believe..." It is the formal confession of faith made by a person or his sponsor at baptism. The Creed is also an essential part of the liturgy through which each person formally and officially renews his/her baptism and membership in the Church. Although the Creed was written originally in the plural "We believe..." because it expresses the faith of the whole Church, the singular "I" is used in baptism and in the Liturgy to express that our faith must also be personal. The Creed begins with the personal pronoun "I" to signify that our faith is personal as well as communal.

St. Paul says in Romans 10:9, "If you confess with your lips that Jesus is Lord and believe in your heart that God raised Him from the dead, you will be saved." How do we "confess" Christ? The Orthodox Church affords us many opportunities to personally confess faith in Christ in the manner prescribed by Paul in Romans. This happens in its prayers, hymns, the Creed, and the liturgical services. Before receiving the Eucharist we pray, "I believe, O Lord, and confess that You are the Christ, the Son of the Living God, Who has come to this world to save sinners, of whom I am the first." Such confessions of faith are deeply personal.

When we confess in the Nicene Creed, for example, "I believe in life everlasting," we must individualize it by using the singular possessive pronoun, "I believe that in Christ my life is everlasting." If the articles of the Creed are not personal, they are not real.

"I" BELIEVE

The purpose of the singular "I" is to challenge each one of us to ask, "Is this really what I believe? It may be my mother's belief, or my father's, or my priest's, but is it mine? Can I claim as mine the articles of faith contained in this Creed that I recite every Sunday? If not, what do I believe? And why? And what are my reasons?"

LIFE'S MOST IMPORTANT RELATIONSHIP

Certain psychologists believe that the condition of our environment the nine months before birth determines what kind of persons we are going to be. Others claim the same importance for the first several years of life after birth. The first two words of the Nicene Creed serve to express our belief as Orthodox Christians that the most significant factor in a person's life is not so much the nine months before birth or the first few years after birth but a person's relationship to God. It is this relationship which determines our destiny for now and for eternity. It is this all-important relationship that is expressed by the words, "I believe." "I believe" not only with my mind but also with my heart and will. "I believe" enough to rest the whole weight of my life with its hopes and fears on Jesus, my Lord and my God.

FOR OUR SALVATION

The Nicene Creed speaks very personally about salvation. It says that it was for our salvation that Jesus came down from heaven. When we see a house on fire on a TV telecast we do not get too excited. But if we see that it is our own house that is on fire, it's a completely different story. We get very excited and do something about it right away. We are personally involved. "Nothing is real until it is local," said G.K. Chesterton.

If the salvation Jesus offers us is to have meaning, if it is to be real, we must come to realize that it is our own house (not someone else's) that is on fire. We must come to see that we are the ones who are in a predicament from which we need to be saved. We must become like the alcoholic or the drug addict when they come to the realization that they have made themselves prisoners and need someone desperately to save them. Unless we experience personally the need for salvation, all this talk about Jesus as Savior will have little or no meaning.

HE WILL JUDGE THE LIVING AND THE DEAD

When we confess in the Nicene Creed that "He (Jesus) will come again to judge the living and the dead," we need to remember that this is a personal statement of faith. It means that I will appear personally before the Lord Jesus one day to give an account to Him of my life. It will be a personal audience, not with the Pope or the Patriarch, but with the Lord God. This is how much God cares for each one of us personally. This is how much what we do in life matters to Him. At the end of life, I will have a personal audience with the Lord Jesus when He comes to judge the living and the dead.

THE TRINITY IS PERSONAL

Some people believe that our belief in the Holy Trinity is highly abstract and impersonal, so much mumbo jumbo. Not so the Church! In her beautiful prayer to the Trinity the all-encompassing personal love of God comes alive:"

> *My hope is the Father.*
> *My refuge is the Son.*
> *My protection is the Holy Spirit.*
> *Blessed Trinity, glory to Thee.*

Is this impersonal? God above us – the Father! God beside us – the Son! God inside us – the Holy Spirit! How personal! How intimate!

I personally derive great strength each day by praying the following very personal prayer to the Trinity:

> *I am loved by God the Father Who created me*
> *out of nothing.*
> *I am loved and redeemed by God the Son, my*
> *Precious Jesus, Who loved me and gave Himself*
> *for me.*
> *I am loved and indwelt by God the Holy Spirit,*
> *God's power and presence within me.*
> *Blessed Trinity, glory to Thee.*

Orthodox Christians believe not because "a God" exists, but because this particular God exists: the Father, the Son, and the Holy Spirit.

> *The grace of our Lord Jesus Christ, and*
> *the love of God the Father,*
> *and the koinonia (fellowship) of*
> *the Holy Spirit be with you now*
> *and forevermore.*

This ancient apostolic blessing which imparts to us the fullness of God is deeply personal. We are invited to pray it every day: "May the grace of our Lord Jesus Christ and the love of God the Father, and the fellowship of the Holy Spirit be with me and all of us today and every day."

Just as Jesus prays for us (as He prayed for Peter), so the Holy Spirit prays for us: "The Spirit Himself intercedes for us with sighs too deep for words" (Romans 8:26). He prays personally for each of us by name.

96

St. Irenaeus pictures the Holy Trinity personally as God the Father stretching His two arms out to us in love; one arm is Jesus and the other arm is the Holy Spirit. So we have Father, Son and Holy Spirit reaching out to us in love. Surely such love demands a response from each one of us. To ignore or reject that Trinitarian love is to miss out on the whole point of life.

THEOLOGY IS PERSONAL

Essentially even theology is personal. Fr. D. Staniloae, the noted Romanian Orthodox theologian, wrote, "Theology is a gift of God which is offered within the context of a personal experience with God and His acts in history."

St. Symeon the New Theologian, for example, was a man of prayer who theologized from profound personal experience, and not from intellectualized theory.

"A theologian is one who truly prays. And one who truly prays is a theologian," wrote Evagrius. One cannot come to know God abstractly or impersonally; for God is a Person. One can come to know Him only through faith and a personal encounter with Him in faith and prayer. One can come to know God only in "the context of a personal experience" with Christ and His acts in the history of our salvation as revealed in the Bible and Sacred Tradition. When we come to know God in this personal way, He will produce "His acts," His signs and wonders in our own life.

Olivier Clement writes about theology and prayer,

> *Prayer and theology are inseparable. True*
> *theology is the adoration offered by the*
> *intellect. The intellect clarifies the movement of*
> *prayer, but only prayer can give it the fervour of*
> *the Spirit. Theology is light, prayer is fire. Their*
> *union expresses the union of the intellect and*
> *the heart. But it is the intellect that must*
> *"repose" in the heart, and theology must*
> *transcend it in love.*[37]

---

37   "The Roots of Christian Mysticism." Olivier Clement. New City Press. 1994.

SPIRITUALITY IS PERSONAL

Spirituality, which seems so vague and abstract, is just another word for our personal relationship with God. Spirituality essentially is the Spirit-filled life of someone, some person, some Christian, some saint, some martyr who had a personal relationship with Christ, who loved Him and whose union with Christ produced a holy life. The whole aim of Orthodox spirituality is the rediscovery of the grace of baptism, the fruits of the seeds God planted in us at baptism, to nourish these seeds and help them grow into a life of holiness.

Even the symbols of our Church are personal and we must view them as such. For example, the acolytes with lighted tapers always precede the Gospel book when it is carried in liturgical procession. This expresses the truth that Christ is the light of the world. But the truth is more personal than that. It means that Jesus provides light for me through the Gospels as I walk through the darkness of this world. When I read His word daily He is indeed very personally "a lamp unto my feet and a light unto my path." The truths expressed by the symbols of our faith are always personal and life-giving.

SIN IS PERSONAL

Just as theology is personal, spirituality is personal, the symbols of the church are personal and existential, so is sin personal. Sin is not the cold, impersonal breaking of a commandment. All sin is sin against love. Our relationship to God is like the intimate relationship of husband and wife. As such, sin is infidelity to love. When we sin, we break not just a commandment; we break God's heart, as the heart of one partner in marriage is broken when the other is unfaithful. Sin is personal unfaithfulness to Christ our Bridegroom. We need to look at the cross and say, "I caused that. My sin crucified Him." Without a strong sense of personal sin, there can be no guilt and no repentance. David expressed this well when he wrote, "I have sinned against You, O God, only against You and done that which is evil in Your sight."

SACRED TRADITION IS PERSONAL

Sacred Tradition, which is such a vital part of our Orthodox faith, is not abstract, but personal. Bishop Ware writes,

Tradition is far more than a set of abstract principles – it is a life, a personal encounter with Christ in the Holy Spirit. Tradition is not only kept by the Church – it lives in the Church. It is the life of the Holy Spirit in the Church... it is not static but dynamic, not a dead acceptance of the past but a living experience of the Holy Spirit in the present.[38]

This means that the Holy Spirit can speak through each one of us to better define the truths of our faith, to protect them, and to share them with the world.

"To many in the twentieth century West," continues Bishop Kallistos Ware, "the Orthodox Church seems chiefly remarkable for its air of antiquity and conservatism; the message of the Orthodox seems to be, 'We are your past.' For the Orthodox themselves, however, loyalty to Tradition means not primarily the acceptance of formulae or customs from past generations, but rather the ever-new, personal and direct experience of the Holy Spirit in the present, here and now."[39]

A LIVING TRADITION

Bishop Ware continues, "Tradition requires us to listen to what the Spirit has said to our predecessors, but it also means listening to the voice of the Spirit in our own day."[40]

Fr. Florovsky loved to say that for us Orthodox the Patristic era is not closed and finished, but has continued down to the present day. The spirit is able in our own time to raise up new Church Fathers and Mothers equal to those in the ancient Church.

The guardian of Sacred Tradition is the total body of the baptized, the "royal priesthood" or "holy nation" (I Peter 2:9) in its entirety, not just the bishops alone but also the laity. That is personal; it includes all of us. We are the guardians and defenders of the faith. According to the well-known Epistle of the Eastern Patriarchs, written in 1849, "The guardian of piety is the very Body of the Church, that is, the people themselves, who will always preserve their faith unchanged."

---

38   "The Orthodox Way." K. Ware. SVS Press. Crestwood, NY. 1979.
39   Ibid.
40   Ibid.

In the early Church there was a meaningful ceremony whereby the faith was entrusted to the laity, and the laity took active responsibility for it. Toward the end of their instruction the candidates for baptism (catechumens) were given the words of the Creed, the "Symbol of the Faith." This ceremony was called "tradition," or the "handing over of the Symbol." Then, immediately before baptism itself, the candidates in turn recited aloud the Creed that had been given to them. This was called the "giving back of the Symbol." In this way, it was made clear that, at baptism, the faith is committed personally to each one of us, and by reciting it aloud we express our responsibility personally to the Savior to keep the faith, uphold it, spread it, and defend it, if need be, at the cost of our lives through the witness of martyrdom. Jesus said, "When the Spirit of truth has come, He will guide you into all truth" (John 16:13). It is this divine promise that forms the basis of the Orthodox devotion to Sacred Tradition. And it includes all of us personally, clergy and laity alike, as members of the Body of Christ, the Church.

Fr. John Meyendorff emphasized the personal aspect of Sacred Tradition when he wrote,

> *I do want to emphasize the point that the mystery of the Holy Spirit, present in the church, is the fundamental reality of Christian experience, that this experience is a personal and free one... Thus the personalism of the faith does not result in charismatic subjectivism or individualism; it initiates each person to think and act as a responsible member of the body seeking the truth within the communion of the saints.*[41]

---

41   "Doing Theology Today." Edited by T.E. McComiskey and J.D. Woodbridge. Zondervan Publishing Company. Grand Rapids, MI. 1992.

Chapter Eleven

The Bible is Personal

Insatiable is the sweetness of spiritual thoughts. Just as the earth that is not watered cannot bring forth wheat even though it may hold within itself thousands of seeds, so also the soul cannot show forth any spiritual fruit unless it is first enlightened by the Holy Scriptures. Again, as wine when drunk helps to put an end to our sorrow and brings gladness to the heart, so also the spiritual wine brings joy to the soul.

– St. John Chrysostom

THE BIBLE IS PERSONAL

A woman once dreamed that she was in the afterlife in a room crowded with grieving people. Suddenly the door opened and Jesus walked in. "My child, why are you crying?" He asked one woman.

"I'm crying, Lord, because my husband died when we were so young, and from then on I was just lost without him. I wanted to serve You, Lord, but I was too lonely and upset all those years to do anything."

"But didn't you get my letter?" asked Jesus.

"What letter, Lord? Did you write a letter?"

"Oh, yes," said Jesus. "I wrote you a letter and told you not to worry, that if you believed in me as you believe in God, I would not leave you comfortless."

The woman looked surprised. "You know," she said, "the priest read from that letter at my husband's funeral, but I didn't know it was personal, from You to me."

A CYNIC AT THE ALTAR

We shall never capture the full meaning of the crucifixion and the resurrection unless we realize that Jesus did all this for us, for each one of us personally.

One Good Friday three cynics walked down a Paris street and saw a long line of people waiting for confession outside a church. Not believing in Christ themselves, they began to make fun of these people. They thought it was all a joke. They dared each other to have one of them stand in line and go in and tell the priest so. One of them accepted the dare. Entering the confessional he said to the priest, "We were walking outside and saw this line of people waiting to come to confession. We think it is all a farce and I agreed to come in and tell you so." The priest replied, "O.K. But I want you to do one thing before you leave. Go in the church. Walk up to the main altar. Look at the body of Christ on the cross and say, 'You died for me, O Christ, but I don't give a damn.' I want you to say this three times. Then you may leave." The cynic walked up to the altar, looked at the body of Christ and with much difficulty said, "You died for me..." and quickly walked away. The priest called him back. "No, you've got to do it two more times. You promised." Hesitantly, he went back, looked at Christ and could not get the words out. Finally he did, "You died for me..." and he quickly ran down the aisle. The priest stopped

102

him. "You promised once more." he said. With even more hesitation he went up to the cross again, stared at it for a long time in pain, then came back to the priest and said, "Father, I am ready for my confession." Who can look at Christ crucified and not say, "God be merciful to me, the sinner"? It is the personal that makes it real.

HE DIED FOR ME

St. Paul knew God's love was personal. That is why he wrote, "The Son of God who loved me and gave Himself for me." This great God put on the robe of human flesh in order to clothe me in the robe of divinity. He took on the form of a slave that He might set me, the slave, free. "He loved me and gave Himself for me." Then St. Paul goes on to say very personally what his life in Christ was all about: "The life I now live in the flesh, I live by faith in the Son of God who loved me and gave Himself for me."

"The Son of God... gave Himself for me." He died for Adam, He died for Judas. He died for John. He died for Mary Magdalene. He died for both thieves who were crucified with Him, even for the bandit who kept cursing Him. But He died also for me, as if His arms were stretched out on the cross only for me. For, He loves us, said St. Augustine, as if there were only one of us in the universe.

God's word assures us that even if a mother were to forget the child of her womb, God will never forget us. Our very name is carved on the palm of His hands, inscribed indelibly in His heart.

"My Lord and my God," said the Apostle Thomas. "I go to my God and your God," said Jesus. How we all need that personal hold upon our Lord!

"I will be their God and they shall be my people," says the Lord (2 Cor 6:16). "My" people, His "chosen" people whom He loves with an everlasting love; whom He purchased not with silver or gold but with the precious blood of His only Son.

The heart of our religion is a personal relationship with God – and we know that relationships thrive on communication. We can't know people intimately by merely being in their presence. It takes conversation to share thoughts and personalities. Christians are meant to have an ongoing conversation with God. We address Him in the language of prayer, and He addresses us in the language of Scripture.

St. Basil said: "The voice of the Gospels is much more magnificent than the other teachings of the Holy Spirit. In the other teachings God spoke to us through his servants the prophets, but in the Gospels He spoke to us personally through His Son and our Lord.

Non-Christian religions have glimpses of God. But they have not looked God in the face in the Person of Jesus in whom all the fullness of God dwells bodily.

SEEING OURSELVES IN THE SCRIPTURES

When we read the Scriptures, we should read them personally. We should see ourselves in them. For example, the blind man groping for the light in John's Gospel – who is he? Myself! Without Christ, I am totally blind! The disciples with their stupid and misguided questions – who are they? Myself! The finical Pharisees with their built-in traditionalism – who are they? Myself!

St. Theophan the Recluse writes,

> *You have a book? Then read it, reflect on what it says, and apply the words to yourself. To apply the content to oneself is the purpose and fruit of reading. If you read without applying what is read to yourself, nothing good will come of it, and even harm may result. Theories will accumulate in the head, leading you to criticize others instead of improving your own life.*

SOME PERSONAL REFLECTIONS

As a priest I always have to contend with what I call an occupational hazard. In my daily Scripture reading it is always a temptation for me to apply to others the insights that the Holy Spirit brings to me. Instead of saying, "The Lord is speaking to me through this powerful verse. I need to apply it to my life. It is meant for my conversion." Instead of applying it to myself, I would apply it to others and plan to use it in my preaching and teaching others. But the word of God is personal It is meant for me first. And if it becomes part of me, I won't even have to preach it verbally; it will shine through my life. "You are the light of the world," said Jesus.

How personally the Prophet Isaiah foretold the sacrifice of the Messiah, "He was wounded for my transgressions. He was bruised for my iniquities. The chastisement that brought about my peace was upon Him, and by His wounds I am healed."

A COLD, IMPERSONAL VIEW OF THE UNIVERSE

Contrast this personal love of God for us with the cold, abstract, impersonal view of life that science offers us. In his book "Dreams of a Final Theory," Nobel-Prize winner Steven Weinberg casts religion in the outer darkness of "wishful thinking." If we stick to science, he says, what we see is a universe that is impersonal and without purpose. This may be a "bleak" and "chilling" view of the world, he says, but it is the only one sanctioned by science.

The world view of Jesus is the exact opposite. Words such as "bleak," "chilling," "abstract," and "impersonal" are all replaced by personal pronouns of love: "Peter, I have prayed for you that you may not fall," said Jesus. The faith and love He demands of us in return are equally personal.

"WHO DO YOU SAY I AM?"

When Jesus asks His disciples, "Who do people say that I am?" they all begin to give replies. "Some say you're this. Others say you're that." But then He gets very personal, "But who do you say that I am?" And that is the very personal question on which our eternal salvation hangs. Not what St. Basil believes about Christ. Not what St. John Chrysostom believes about Christ. But what do I believe about Him? Who is He for me? Is He is *my* Lord? Is He *my* God?

"MY GOSPEL"

It is interesting to note that sometimes St. Paul called his faith "the gospel." At other times, "the gospel of God" or "the gospel of Christ." But sometimes he calls it, "my gospel." And that's what helped Paul through his many hardships. Not just the gospel but "my gospel." He believed in Jesus, the Son of God, Who "loved me and gave Himself for me."

God, even when believed in, can be many things to many people. To some people He can be as far off as the rings of Saturn. To others, He is merely the One Who made the constellations. But to others He can be like an inner spring or well in a person's soul. As Jesus said to the woman of Samaria, "The water that I shall give you will become in you a well of water springing up to eternal life."

This is the God we need to come to know personally – the God Who is not just a theory to explain the universe, abstract, far away, impersonal, but the God Who is an inner well, an inner presence as real as bread, and as refreshing as water, sustaining and upholding us in the darkest of days. "The reading of Holy Scripture is the opening of heaven," said St. John Chrysostom.

To get a taste of how personal God's word is, turn to I Cor. 13, the love chapter. Read it aloud, placing your name wherever the word "love" is mentioned (I Cor 13:4-7). When God pours His love in us through the Holy Spirit, do we not become love?

I remember the story of a Chinese man whose name was Lo. When he heard missionaries read from Matthew 28:20: "And, lo, I am with you always, even unto the end of the world," his heart leaped for joy. "Just think," he said, "the Lord knows my name and makes me a promise like that!"

We need to remember that the Lord has made the same personal promise to each one of us: "And __(your name)__, I am with you always, even unto the end of the world."

We need to place our name in each of God's promises.

WHY THE BIBLE DOES NOT ATTEMPT TO PROVE GOD

Nowhere do the Bible writers ever attempt to prove the existence of God. God was so real to them that having to prove His existence would be like trying to prove that one's mother exists. They knew God by experience. They felt His presence in their lives every day. They felt no need to prove the existence of the obvious.

READ EXPECTANTLY

When a rich member of a family died, all the relatives were called together by a lawyer for the reading of the will. As it was being read, each person listened intently, expectantly, eagerly, waiting to hear his/her name mentioned. One older person, who had difficulty hearing, brought along an old hearing horn and placed it in his ear so that he might not miss a single word.

This is a picture of how expectantly we should be listening when God speaks. Everything He says is directed personally to us. We stand to inherit a kingdom. Everything He promises has our name on it. That is why we hear the command "proshomen" – or "Let us be attentive" – so often in the liturgy just before a Scripture reading. It means "Listen!" "Pay attention now." The Lord is about to speak to you personally.

SACRAMENTAL POWER

The Bible is not just another book. It is a sacrament. It is a personal love letter from God to you, containing a proposal for marriage. Jesus is the Bridegroom, you are the bride. He wishes to enter into the most intimate possible relationship of love with you. He delivers a marriage proposal to you through the Holy Bible. It is marked R.S.V.P. He expects a response. It is the most important response you will ever make in your life. Will you say "yes" or "no" to your Creator, your Savior, your Bridegroom, your God? Your eternal destiny will depend on that personal response.

Bishop Kallistos Ware writes about the Bible, "As a book uniquely inspired by God and addressed to each of the faithful personally, the Bible possesses sacramental power, transmitting grace to the reader, bringing him to a point of meeting and decisive encounter (with God)."

The Bible is the real presence of Christ. It is not an ancient text to be read with the mind. It is Christ speaking to you personally. Fr. George Florovsky once said, "No one profits by the Gospels unless he is first in love with Christ. For Christ is not a text but a living Person, and He abides in His Body, the Church."

In John, Chapter 17:6-9, Jesus prays fervently and specifically for His disciples through the ages, those He would leave behind to continue His work in His absence and for those who would succeed them. And that means He was praying for you and me. And Jesus is still praying for you and me. Someone said, "If I could hear Christ praying for me in the next room, I would not fear a million enemies. Yet distance makes no difference. He is in the next room praying for me."

PERSONAL APPLICATION

Bishop Kallistos Ware writes about applying God's word personally to ourselves,

According to Saint Mark the Monk ("Mark the Ascetic," fifth/sixth century), "he who is humble in his thoughts and engaged in spiritual work, when he reads the Holy Scriptures, will apply everything to himself and not to his neighbor." We are to look throughout Scripture for a personal application. Our question is not simply "What does it mean?" but "What does it mean for me?" As Saint Tikhon insists, "Christ Himself is speaking to you." Scripture is a direct, intimate dialogue between the Saviour and myself – Christ addressing me and my heart responding.

Thus, as we read God's word, we need to ask ourselves some very personal questions:

    a. What does the Scripture say?
    b. What does the Scripture say to me?
    c. How does my life compare with the Scripture?
    d. What definite steps am I going to take to line up my life with the Scripture?

PERSONALIZING THE WORD OF GOD

When we read the Bible, we should personalize it by placing our name in every promise. Let us take John 3:16 as an example. When it is personalized, it reads,

> *God so loved me, (name), that He gave His only Son, so that I, (name), who believes in Him, may not perish but have eternal life.*
>
> *– (Jn 3:16)*

Other Bible promises are already personal and need to be claimed personally by us. Here are some:

> *Fear not, (name), for I am with you, be not dismayed, for I am your God*
>
> *I will strengthen you (name), I will help you, (name),*

I will uphold you (name), with my victorious right hand.

I, (name), sought the Lord, and He answered me, and delivered me from all my fears. Look to Him, and be radiant" (Ps 34:4,5)

My God shall supply all your needs according to riches in glory in Christ Jesus (St. Paul).

Notice that St. Paul does not say just God – some God, any God – but he says, *my* God. And he doesn't say that his God *can* supply all his needs but *shall* supply all his needs. So, it is my privilege to take this glorious promise, claim it, appropriate it, affirm it, and say, "My God shall supply all my needs according to His riches in glory in Christ Jesus."

TEKNIA: MY LITTLE CHILDREN

St. Nicodemos of the Holy Mountain wrote:

In John 13:33 the Lord does not refer to His Apostles as sons, but rather in a more tender, more authentic and familiar manner. He calls them teknia – "little children," something He never called them before: "Little children, yet a little while I am with you" (Jn 13:33). Oh, what great and tender love you have for us, dearest Jesus, most compassionate and lover of mankind.

The word *teknia* in Greek is an intimately warm and personal word that translates as "my dear little children." If Jesus addressed His apostles with this beautiful word, will He not address us – His contemporary apostles – in the same manner?

AN INHERITANCE... RESERVED FOR YOU

St. Peter writes of an imperishable inheritance reserved in heaven especially for you:

Blessed be the God and Father of our Lord Jesus Christ! By His great mercy He has given us a new birth into a living hope through the resurrection of Jesus Christ from the dead, and

*into an inheritance that is imperishable,
undefiled, and unfading, reserved in heaven for
you...*

(I Peter 1:3-4)

Is it any wonder that St. Basil urges us to "read the Scriptures for your own sake, for you will find there the remedy for every one of your ailments."

THE PSALMS ARE PERSONAL

If you wish to know how personal your relationship with God can be, read the Psalms. Personally, I love the Psalms! No matter how often I read them, I never get bored. Always, some new insight speaks to my heart and its needs for the day. The Psalms make me feel so human. In them I find another heart that understands and touches mine. Another mortal has felt before, what I'm going through now; what I'm feeling now.

The Psalmist had a person-to-person relationship with God. He held nothing back from God. He laid everything out before Him, his "ups" and his "downs," his exaltations and his despair. He told God everything; even getting angry with Him at times.

Listen to Psalm 23:

> *The Lord is my shepherd,
> I shall not want.
> He makes me to lie down in green pastures:
> He leads me beside the still waters.
> He restores my soul...*

Someone described the psalms as "the outpouring of the heart to God in the most intimate personal communion... springing out of the needs and aspirations of the soul in the crises of life."

Listen as David pours out his sorrow to God so very personally in Psalm 51:

> *Be merciful to me, God, because of your
> constant love; wipe away my sins, because of
> your great mercy! Wash away my evil, and make
> me clean from my sin!*

I recognize my faults; I am always conscious of my sins. I have sinned against you – only against you, and done what you consider evil. So you are right in judging me; you are justified in condemning me. I have been evil from the time I was born, from the day of my birth I have been sinful.

A faithful heart is what you want; fill my mind with your wisdom. Remove my sin, and I will be clean; wash me, and I will be whiter than snow. Let me hear the sound of joy and gladness; and though you have crushed and broken me, I will be happy once again. Close your eyes to my sins, and wipe out all my evil.

Create a pure heart in me, God, and put a new and loyal spirit in me. Do not banish me from your presence; do not take your holy spirit away from me. Give me again the joy that comes from your salvation, and make my spirit obedient. Then I will teach sinners your commands, and they will turn back to you.

Spare my life, God my Savior, and I will gladly proclaim your righteousness.

Help me to speak, Lord, and I will praise you.

You do not want sacrifices, or I would offer them; you are not pleased with burnt offerings. My sacrifice is a submissive spirit, God; a submissive and obedient heart you will not reject.

God, be kind to Zion and help her; rebuild the walls of Jerusalem. Then you will be pleased with the proper sacrifices, and with all burnt offerings; and calves will be sacrificed on your altar.

Since God does not change, we, too, can enjoy the same relationship with Him as David or Paul or Abraham or Moses. We can choose to have a very open, loving, personal relationship with Him. Or, we can choose to keep Him at arm's length and "go it alone," rootless, hopeless, restless, incredibly lonely. The choice is ours.

Chapter Twelve

Relating Our Faith
Personally to Others in Love

Someone said once, "If you want to fill a dozen milk bottles, you must not stand back and spray them with a hose. You can get them wet, but you won't fill them. You must take them one by one."

RELATING OUR FAITH PERSONALLY TO OTHERS IN LOVE

If we truly believe that God loves each one of us personally, then our faith will translate into a deeply personal love for God's living images: His children. Through the grace of the Holy Spirit, we are empowered to relate to others on a personal, one-on-one, I-Thou level, and thus make real to all the intimately personal love of God.

A certain author tells how he personalizes his love for his wife. Once a week they go out to dinner alone so that they may have time to look deeply into each other's eyes and soul. And each day they spend fifteen minutes visiting in depth, listening to each other, sharing their mutual hopes, surfacing their hostilities, discussing their worries, praying together. If we make time for such deeply personal encounters, we shall discover a wonderful way to keep love alive and growing.

To express this personal love, one father takes each child out to dinner alone every month. Often it's just for a hamburger. Father and son or daughter sit down alone and discuss whatever is on their minds. Mostly dad listens to junior's troubles. Can you think of a better way to make parental love more personal?

Many parishes sponsor small study and prayer groups. The purpose of these groups is to make the love of Christ more personal. When ten or twelve people meet together in a circle of prayer and Bible study, they begin to sense that they are members "one of another." The love of Christ becomes personal in the sharing and praying of such small groups.

AS IF DELIVERED TO A SINGLE INDIVIDUAL

No sermon or instruction can be truly effective unless it is delivered to a single individual. Ideally, the teacher should have only one student. This emphasis on the one-to-one relationship between master and disciple, and the requirement that the master lead the student down a path he has already traversed, shows that the teacher is called to teach with more than just words. He is called to be a model for the student, a paradigm.

The most effective teaching is accomplished on the personal one-to-one level.

A PERSONAL MENTOR

Much emphasized in Orthodox spirituality is the importance of having a mentor, a spiritual father or mother, as one grows in Christ.

Called *geron* in Greek, and *starets* in Russian, what this spiritual mentor offers is not so much a rule of prayer or a set of moral instructions as a one-on-one personal relationship. There is magic in a personal relationship that is nourished and energized by the Holy Spirit. Things happen, changes are effected, when we engage in a personal I-Thou encounter that is under the guidance of the Holy Spirit.

The geron/staretz mentor tradition in the Orthodox Church testifies to the fact that a life that is just "Jesus and me" is incomplete and will not progress very far. Our personal relationship with Christ needs to be anchored in the Church, and it flowers when it seeks the advice of a spiritual mentor or geron on a one-on-one basis.

TWO EXAMPLES

Following are two examples of such one-on-one love. Incident number one: An old lady was scrubbing the stairs of an Anglican cathedral in London. She fell into conversation with a priest. "Do you know the Archbishop of Canterbury?" she asked. "Yes, I do," was the reply. "Well, you know," said the scrubwoman, "he came here the other day. And he asked me how I was, because he said I didn't look happy. And I told him that I couldn't be happy, with two sons in a prison camp in Germany, and the old man not able to work, and me having to work for him, and not much to live on. And do you know what His Grace did? He sat down on that step there, listened to me for an hour as we talked about God."

The second incident is from the life of the late Pope John the 23rd. A husband once stopped him and asked him to pray for his wife who was seriously ill at home. He said to the man, "Gladly! I'll not only pray for her, but I'll go home with you right now to visit and pray for her personally." He got into the Pope's car and they drove to the man's house.

INDIVIDUAL ATTENTION

We all like individual attention. That's why we respond favorably to anyone who singles us out and focuses his attention directly on us. When first baseman Darrell Evans became a free agent after the 1983 season, he was sought by several teams. But he decided to sign with the Detroit Tigers because, as he said, "Sparky Anderson was the only manager interested enough to call me and talk personally!"

THE MAGIC OF LOVE

The magic of personal love works miracles as this true story testifies:

> *Even one person's intimate love can deeply heal another. For example, Tom, a simple person without training in psychotherapy, worked as an orderly in a mental hospital. One of the sickest patients in the hospital, a deeply psychotic woman, had been there for eighteen years. She never spoke to anyone, or even looked in another's eyes. She sat alone all day in a rocking chair, rocking back and forth. One day during his dinner break, Tom found another rocking chair, pulled it over, and rocked along beside her as he ate his dinner. He returned the next day, and the next. Tom worked only five days per week, but he asked for special permission to come in on his days off so he could rock with the psychotic woman. Tom did this every day for six months. Then one evening as he got up to leave, the woman said, "Good night." It was the first time she had spoken in eighteen years. After that, she began to get well. Tom still came to rock with her every day, and eventually she was healed of her psychosis.*[42]

As Christians we have the world's greatest message – Jesus died and rose again personally for you and me. This gospel message translates into a love that heals. We must present this message as personally as Jesus did to the Samaritan woman and to so many others.

THE PERSONAL SAVES

Thomas Merton said once, "In the end, it is the reality of personal relationships that saves everything." This is especially true of our relationship with God.

---

42   "Healing the Eight Stages of Life." M. Linn, S. Fabricant, D. Linn. Paulist Press. 1988.

When we look at Christ crucified on the Cross personally for you and for me, we cannot but utter the words of a penitent sinner who wrote:

> *If I had been less proud, the crown of thorns*
> *would have been less piercing. If I had been less*
> *avaricious and greedy, His hands would have*
> *been dug less by the steel. If I had been less*
> *sensual, His flesh would not be hanging from*
> *Him like purple rags. If I had not wandered*
> *away like a lost sheep, in the perversity of my*
> *egotism, His feet would have been less riven*
> *with nails. I am sorry, not just because I broke a*
> *law: I am sorry because I wounded Him Who*
> *died out of love for me."*

THE MAGIC OF THE PERSONAL

What a wonderful change takes place in people when they are treated in a personal way. Those who truly love you and care for you become totally present to you when they are in your presence. When they listen, they are listening to you with their whole being. Their eyes are there only for you. Their ears are there only for you. When they speak, you know they are speaking only to you. When they ask questions, you know that it is for your sake and not for their own. Their presence is a healing presence because it is completely personal. Magic changes take place in us when we are in such a presence.

ON BEING COMPLETELY PRESENT

Mark Van Doren said once:

"There is one thing we can do, and the happiest people are those who do it to the limit of their ability.

"We can be completely present. We can be all there. We can control the tendency of our minds to wander from the situation we are in, toward yesterday, toward tomorrow, toward something we have forgotten, toward some other place we are going next. It is hard to do this, but it is harder to understand afterward wherein it was we fell so short. It was where and when we ceased to give our entire attention to the person, the opportunity before us.

"Those who have fewest regrets are those who take each moment as it comes for all that it is worth. It will never come again, for worse or better. It is ours alone; we can make it what we will."

A truly great example of being completely present is our Lord Jesus Christ who was always completely present to people. To mention just a few instances, He notices Zacchaeus hidden up in a tree and invites him to have dinner with him. He hears the call of the blind beggar by the roadside and responds with healing. He hears the cry of the penitent thief on the cross and says, "Today you will be with me in paradise."

How often people come to us, children to parents, wives to husbands, friends to friends, trying to unload their burdens, and as we sit there listening, our minds and hearts are thousands of miles away. If we were completely present to each other, we would rightfully expect miracles to happen. To be completely present to others is to help them experience the personal love of God.

DEPERSONALIZING OTHERS

Dr. Paul Tournier tells of an experience of a Dr. Plattner, a friend of his. A woman came to him seeking an abortion. Always she referred to the child she wished destroyed as "a little collection of cells." She had completely devalued and depersonalized the child. Then one day Dr. Plattner had an idea. "What name would you give the child," he asked, "if it were to be born?" The atmosphere of the conversation changed. The woman was silent; one felt that the child, as soon as she gave him a name in her own mind, was ceasing to be "a little collection of cells," in order to become a person... "It was staggering," concluded Dr. Plattner. "I felt as if I had been present at an act of creation."

I remember a medical doctor who said once, "I have never had an expectant mother come to me and ask, 'How is my fetus doing?'"

Science has a way of depersonalizing the unborn child by calling him or her an "embryo" or a "fetus." Yet the very word embryo comes from two Greek words meaning "child within." Fetus comes from the Latin and means "little one."

Someone said once, "In this society, we save timber, wolves, bald eagles and coke bottles. Yet everyone wanted me to throw away my baby."

It is easier to kill when one depersonalizes someone whether it be an embryo or an enemy soldier. A young American stationed in a missile silo said once, "I don't know if I can kill someone up close. This way I just press a button and I never have to see whom my missile hits." It is lifegiving when we treat someone as a person; it is deadly when we depersonalize people.

THE NEW STAMP MACHINE

An elderly Scottish lady went to her village post office one morning. In the lobby a workman was busy installing some kind of machine. When she got to the window she asked for her stamps, and then added, "What is that thing you are putting in the lobby?" With a smile of pride the postmaster replied, "That's our new stamp machine. You won't have to stand in line any longer. You will put in your money and out will come the stamps." The Scottish lady eyed the machine a bit quizzically for a moment and then asked a profound question: "But tell me, will it ask about my rheumatism?"

Machines are fine but they are impersonal. They don't ask about your rheumatism.

THE "ANCHOR MAN"

Recently I read the story of a person who had to go through the Mayo Clinic in Rochester, Minnesota. It impressed me because it illustrates how personal we can make our concern for others. After being admitted to the Clinic, this man said, he was ushered into a doctor's small office. Each patient at Mayo is assigned to a doctor who becomes his "anchor man" regardless of how many other specialists he sees. The doctor came in, introduced himself, and said, "This is a big place. You may feel lost here. But I want you to know that every facility of the Clinic is here for one purpose – to serve you." He took out a card, wrote down a number and said, "If you need me any hour of the day or night while you are here, pick up the phone in your room, call this number, and I'll be at your side within five minutes." The patient went on to say, "That did something for me. I felt that I was not part of an impersonal machine; I was the most important element here. I knew that someone cared. Already, I felt better."

As I read this story I thought, "Isn't that exactly the kind of love we Christians should have?" Our love for people should be personal – deeply personal – at least as personal as what that Mayo doctor gave his patient.

Chapter Thirteen

Personal Encounters with God

With my exposure to Orthodoxy and to
Orthodox people, a new idea began to enter
my awareness: that Truth was not just an
abstract idea, sought and known by the mind,
but was something personal – even a Person –
sought and loved by the heart. And that is
how I met Christ.

– By a Convert to the Orthodox Church

PERSONAL ENCOUNTERS WITH GOD

It is interesting to note that it was the pagan world that called Jesus' disciples "Christians," meaning followers of Christ. Jesus did not call His disciples "Christians." He called them "witnesses." Jesus could have said, "You are my lawyers." But a lawyer is always presenting an argument. He is debating and reasoning whereas a witness simply tells what he knows from personal experience. And we know that an argument from one's personal experience is irrefutable.

If we have developed a personal relationship with our Master, we cannot but become effective witnesses for Him in the world. The mouth will always speak out of the abundance and overflow of the heart. This is especially true for parents, teachers, and priests. We are not God's lawyers speaking with contrived arguments; we are His witnesses speaking and teaching out of the abundance of our hearts. We speak of that which we have seen and heard and experienced.

THEOLOGY IN THE CONTEXT OF WORSHIP

This is reflected in how theology is taught in the Orthodox Church. Unlike most schools of theology of the West, which are so often merely rational and intellectual enterprises, theology in the Eastern Church grows out of prayer and worship. True theology occurs, according to the Church Fathers, within the context of faith, godliness, and worship. In other words, theology grows from the experiential, from the personal experience of God in prayer and worship. "The true theologian is one who truly prays," say the Church Fathers. This is why many of the Orthodox seminaries traditionally have been attached to monasteries where daily prayer, morning and evening, is the rule and where each novice is under the mentorship of an elder, geronta or staretz, with a one-on-one spiritual tutorship.

THE EXPERIENCE OF GOD IN THE BIBLE

This reflects the experience of God's people in the Bible. The Bible is not primarily a record of people's thoughts about God, but a record of their actual experiences of God. No wonder its pages are filled with such sublime personal statements as, "I know that my Redeemer lives" (Job); "I know, and am persuaded that He is able to keep that which I have committed unto Him against that day" (St. Paul). They lived through trials and were given strength. Their souls were in peril, and God led them into secure places. They said these things, not because they were taught, but because they had experienced them, they were *martyres*, eye witnesses. Their faith was personal.

What people want to hear is not God's lawyers presenting logical arguments for His existence but God's witnesses sharing from personal experience what God has done for them. And this is what the early Christians were: witnesses, *martyres*. As someone said of the early Christians: "God? They knew Him! Miracles? They themselves were miracles! Resurrection? They had gone through it! Heaven? They were living in it! Hell? They had escaped it! Reconciliation? They rejoiced in it! Eternal Life? They possessed it!" It was all very personal.

TAPE RECORDER TO TAPE RECORDER

Bishop Kallistos Ware said once,

> *In today's dehumanized world, in which we anticipate hell by no longer looking in any profound sense at each other's faces, one of our most important tasks as Christians is to reaffirm the supreme value of direct personal communion. We must not allow the machines to take over, as happens in the anecdote about the psychiatrist and his new patient, "It's easier for me to concentrate," said the psychiatrist at their first meeting, "if I'm not actually looking at you. So I'll sit over there in the corner behind you as you lie down on the couch and tell me your story." After a time the patient grew suspicious, for it was curiously quiet behind the curtain in the corner. So he tiptoed across the room, and his misgivings were confirmed. He saw behind the curtain a door, and near it a chair, but there was no psychiatrist on the chair – only a tape-recorder. The man was not unduly perturbed, for he had related his story many times to different psychiatrists, and he had it all down on tape. He took a tape-recorder out of his brief-case, laid it on the couch, and turned*

*it on. Then he went downstairs and across the road
to a coffee shop. Inside he found the psychiatrist,
already drinking coffee; so the man ordered his
own cup of coffee and sat down at the same table.
"Look here," the psychiatrist protested, "you're
not supposed to be here. You should be upstairs on
the couch telling your story." "Don't worry," the
man replied. "My tape-recorder's talking to your
tape-recorder."*

*As Christians we are here to insist on the vital
need for unmediated personal encounter: not
machine to machine, but face to face, person to
person, prosopon to prosopon, according to the
model of God the Trinity.*[43]

Our relationship to God, our prayer life must be personal, face to
face, not mechanical, not impersonal, not "tape recorder to tape recorder,"
saying certain prayers by rote, which Jesus condemned when He talked
about the people who honor God only with their lips, but their hearts are
far from Him.

Dr. Christos Yannaras states that the Greek word for person, prosopon,
has the literal meaning of "face": I am authentically a person only in so
far as I "face" others, especially God, and relate to them personally.
▬▬▬▬▬▬▬▬▬▬▬▬▬▬▬▬▬▬▬▬▬▬▬▬▬▬▬▬▬▬▬▬▬▬ Not so
among humans who are designed to face each other in this sacred act of
procreation which is blessed by God in the Sacrament of Holy Matri-
mony. Love among humans is designed by God to be expressed face to
face, person to person, in the most intimate of all relationships.

In the Old Testament God did not have a face. Moses was allowed
to see only God's "backside." In the New Testament God has a face in
the Person of Jesus. Thus, we are invited to relate to Him face to face,
person to person, personally and intimately.

EXAMPLES OF PERSONS WHOSE FAITH WAS PERSONAL

ARCHBISHOP ANASTASIOS YANNOULATOS is an eminent
spiritual leader of the Orthodox Church. He is presently the spiritual

---

43   "Personhood." Edited by John Chirban. Bergin and Garvey Co. 1995.

leader of the Orthodox Church in Albania. He has served as missionary to Africa while he was at the same time professor at the University of Athens. He is the Father of the modern missionary movement in Greece.

During World War II young Yannoulatos began to experience his faith in a very personal way. Abandoning his interest in mathematics, he pursued theology and graduated from the University of Athens in 1951 with highest honors. He did post-graduate work in Germany where he earned a doctorate. So fervent was his love for Jesus that he said, "It was not enough for me to give something to God. I had to be given totally to Him. I wanted to live with my whole being in Christ." He dedicated his life to making the Orthodox faith real to his people. For Archbishop Yannoulatos, ministry began when his faith in Jesus became personal.

METROPOLITAN ANTHONY BLOOM says that his personal relationship with Jesus began when he was a student in medical school. One evening as he was reading the Gospel of Mark, he felt the living presence of Jesus in his room. It was an experience that changed his life. From that moment on, his faith in Jesus began to be deeply personal. And we know how beautifully personal it is when we read his inspiring books on prayer.

ST. KOSMAS AITOLOS was a missionary who traveled the villages of Greece during the dark centuries of Turkish occupation, preaching Christ everywhere he went. Arriving at each village square, he would ask the people to set up a large wooden cross in the village square. Placing a bench in front of the cross, he stood on the bench and preached extemporaneously on the love of God and the teachings of Jesus. Then he would travel to the next village, leaving the cross in its place as a reminder of his teachings to the villagers.

Kosmas' faith was nourished by a deeply personal and intimate relationship to Jesus Whom he called "our sweetest Master" and "our sweetest Jesus." God's love overflowed Kosmas' heart. Here is a sample of what he would say,

> *The most gracious and merciful God has many and various names. He is called light, life, and resurrection. But God's chief name is love. If we wish to live well here and go to paradise, we should have two loves: love for God and love for our brethren... Just as a swallow needs two wings to fly in the air so do we need these two*

loves (love of God and love of people) because
without them it is impossible for us to be saved.

AN IMPERSONAL WORLD

We live in a society in which we are identified by numbers. We are a social security number to the government. Another number identifies us at our place of employment. We are a number in college and a number in the armed forces. We are told that computer cards can translate all of our personality traits into numerical digits by which we can be sorted and identified. We are told that one day we may receive mail addressed to our social security number, followed by street number and finally a zip code.

One person examined his billfold and discovered that he carried credit cards and identification numbers totaling twenty-one different sets of numbers by which he was known. We can sympathize with the person who said, "I have finally learned how to get attention. When I receive a computer card, I fold, spindle and mutilate it. Then it stops the whole machine, and they learn my name and discover I am a person."

Dr. Paul Tournier said once, "The more we fill our universe with machines, the more important it is that we treat each other as persons."

A successful defense attorney was asked once how he managed to win so often in court. He replied, "I tell the jury about Tom Jones or Bill Green. I never refer to them as 'the defendant' or 'my client.' I've found that juries will hang defendants and clients but that they are not so anxious to hang Tom Jones or Bill Green." This successful attorney had discovered the importance of the personal.

THE GREATNESS OF GOD

Mrs. Humphrey Ward, the British novelist, once wrote to a member of Parliament telling him of the great needs of a family among his constituents. She asked him to give the family his attention. He replied that he was so busy with the human race that he had no time for the individual. That night Mrs. Ward wrote in her diary, "Our Divine Lord, when last heard from, had not attained this sublime attitude." The greatness of our God is that even through He rules the universe, He has time for, and listens to, and cares for each one of His children individually and personally.

The Lord Jesus demonstrated many times that He thinks of us not as crowds, or masses but as persons and individuals. We repeat: He loves us as if there were only one of us in this universe. And as far as He is concerned there is only one of us because each one of us is unique. In this vast universe there is no one exactly like us. The very hairs of our head are numbered and known to God. He calls us by name. And He is concerned about each of our needs. If Christ's ministry among us had any purpose, it was to demonstrate His personal love for us. Jesus made God's love personal:

> *to friendless Zacchaeus sitting alone up in a tree;*
>
> *to the blind beggar lying by the roadside, crying for help;*
>
> *to the woman who touched the hem of His robe seeking healing;*
>
> *to the adulteress who was about to be stoned for her sin;*
>
> *to the father who came pleading in behalf of his sick daughter;*
>
> *to the thief who was crucified next to him;*
>
> *and to the Samaritan woman whom He met by the well.*

His days and hours were full yet He was never too busy to spend time with individuals to show them that God cared personally for each one of them.

When a woman touched Him in a crowd one day, Jesus asked, "Who touched me?" His disciples were often in crowds that meant little to them. They were amazed at His question and said, "In all this crowd you want to know who touched you?" But Jesus didn't want anyone to get lost in a crowd. He didn't want anyone to be treated impersonally.

How much we need to make the love of Christ personal to people today. It was said of a great preacher that each person in his audience felt as though the message was intended for him and for him alone. Each day we need to throw one arm up vertically to receive Christ's love and throw the other arm out horizontally to aim this love to other people.

One of the most personal encounters Jesus had was with the Samaritan woman at the well.

A PERSONAL ENCOUNTER

"There came a woman of Samaria to draw water. Jesus said to her, 'Give me a drink.'" Notice that Jesus doesn't approach the Samaritan woman brandishing a Bible and talking of repentance. He just asks for a drink of water. He does not act superior to her but as inferior. She has something which He needs: water.

The conversation that develops begins in a very informal way, but before it is finished it has covered some of the deepest questions of morals and theology. But the really important thing is not the content of the conversation – significant as that is – as much as the extremely personal encounter that is taking place. This is a real person who has met Jesus, and Jesus gives her His whole attention. She is as real as any of us. And she has met someone unique – one who seems to look right into her depths and knows all about her. "Come and see a man who has told me everything I ever did," she said to her fellow villagers. She came to know Jesus personally as a result of this tremendous I-Thou encounter she had with Him.

Don't we all need such a personal encounter with Jesus in order for our faith to grow? Is not this what Jesus offers us in prayer, in the daily reading of His word, in the Jesus Prayer, in the praying of the daily hours, in the Eucharist? He sits at the well which is called prayer or scripture or the Eucharist and waits for us to come to Him so that we may have a personal, life-changing encounter with Him. The more personal our encounter with Jesus, the more real our faith becomes.

JACOB: STRUGGLE WITH GOD

We read in the Old Testament that Jacob wrestled with God (Gen. 32:23-31). We are to understand from this story that a great thing happened in the life of Jacob. Somewhere in his career he underwent a conversion, an experience with God. At the same point in his life this ambitious man was truly blessed and touched by God's grace. As a result of this very personal experience with God his life was changed. The new name, Israel, given to Jacob at this point signifies the new person he became.

128

Just as Jacob had a personal "struggle" with God, a personal encounter with Him, so each one of us must meet Christ personally, usually through some struggle, and decide for Him at some point in life.

THE RABBIT AND THE DOGS

The following story comes from the Sayings of the Desert Fathers:

Abba Hilarion [founder of Palestinian monasticism] was asked, "How can it be right for a diligent brother not to be offended when he sees other monks returning to the world?" The old man said, "Let me tell you a story. Consider the hunting dogs which chase after hares; imagine one of these dogs sees a hare in the distance and immediately gives chase; the other dogs that are with him see this dog taking off and take off after him, even through they have not seen the hare. They will continue running with him, but only for a time; when at length the effort and struggle exhaust them, they give up the chase and turn back. However the dog that saw the hare continues chasing it by himself. He does not allow the effort or the struggle to hinder him from completing his long course. He risks his life as he goes on, giving himself no rest. He does not allow the turning aside of the other dogs behind him to put him off. He goes on running until he has caught the hare he saw. He is careless both of the stumbling blocks in his path, whether stones or thorns, and of the wounds they have inflicted on him. So also the brother who wishes to follow after Christ must fix his gaze upon the cross until he catches up with Him that was crucified upon it, even though he sees everyone else has begun to turn back."

If we have experienced God personally in Christ; if we have experienced His resurrection, His forgiveness, His love, His grace, His peace, His joy, then like that dog that had actually seen the rabbit, we shall not easily drop out of the race of life; we shall persevere in the faith, until one day we stand in His presence and hear Him calling us by name, " your name , come inherit the kingdom prepared for you from the foundation of the world."

FROM EMPTINESS TO FULLNESS

An executive who had achieved success in the business world wrote, "The success came, all right, but something was missing. I felt a terrible emptiness. I was running on empty. Sometimes I would get up on the middle of the night and pace the floor of my bedroom and stare out into the darkness for hours at a time. I would go to the office and do my job, but there was a big hole in my life. One day I saw what was missing: God! I went back to Church, became an active member, turned my life over to Jesus and established a deeply personal relationship with Him. Now I feel His presence with me, His peace within me. I can sense His Spirit in me. I have come from emptiness to fullness."

In no other religion does a believer enter into a personal relationship with God as in Christianity. It is this personal relationship with Christ that is decisive. Unlike Buddhism, Confucianism or Mohamedanism, Christianity demands a personal, intimate bond and union with Christ. We have to be one with Him; one with Him in such a way that we cannot in any way claim to be Christian unless we reflect the person, the mind, the will, the heart, and the humanity of Jesus. "I live, yet not I, but Christ lives in me," said St. Paul.

BLAISE PASCAL

Dr. Blaise Pascal has been called the greatest mind that ever lived. In his book "A Short History of the Life of Jesus Christ" he wrote, "At midnight 23 November 1654, Jesus spoke to me and said, 'Blaise, I was thinking of thee in my agony.'" This experience caused Pascal to be converted. It made the crucifixion personal. "Blaise" said the voice of Christ, "it was for you I did all this." Jesus suffered, died, was buried, and rose again not for humanity in general but for each one of us personally. When we realize and accept this, our whole life changes.

WHAT A PERSONAL RELATIONSHIP WITH GOD WILL YIELD

Developing a strong daily, personal relationship with Christ will help us accomplish at least five goals in life:

1. It will help us grow in our faith.

2. It will help us experience personally the presence, the love and the power of God; making us *martyres*, effective witnesses for Him in the world.

3. It will fill us to overflowing with the love of God, enabling us to create communities of love at home, at work, at church.

4. St. Irenaeus said, "Communion with God is life. Separation from God is death." Developing a daily personal relationship with Christ will enhance our communion with God and fill us with life – God's life.

5. If the liturgy seems stale, the sacraments empty rituals, I try to get to know Jesus. He helps me see that He is at the center of every liturgy and sacrament, offering Himself to me in love. If the Bible sounds more like bad news than good news, I try to get to know Jesus. Then I find that the Bible is Christ speaking personally to me words of everlasting live. If I find Church on Sunday a chore, I try to get to know Jesus more personally. Then I find I want to come to meet Him personally in the liturgy and receive Him in the manger of my soul. There is no substitute for getting to know Jesus personally and learning to love Him faithfully. When this happens, everything comes alive.

A LITTLE BLACK GIRL'S PERSONAL FAITH

When a little black North Carolina girl was being escorted to school by soldiers in 1962, she said, "I was all alone, and those (segregationist) people were screaming at me. Suddenly I saw God smiling at me, and I smiled back." She continued, "A woman was standing there (near the school door), and she shouted at me, 'Hey, you little nigger, what you smiling at?' I looked right at her face and I said, 'At God.' Then she looked up at the sky, and then she looked at me, and she didn't call me any more names."

This little black girl had a warm personal relationship with Jesus that sustained her with an inner equanimity and peace which was nothing less than God's presence in her. God smiled the blessing of His presence and love upon her, and she smiled back!

AN ETERNAL HONEYMOON WITH JESUS

To understand how deeply personal God's love is, I bring to your attention what one church father said about his impending death. He said that he looked forward to death as intensely as a young groom looks forward to being with his bride on the first night of their wedding. For him death was to be the beginning of an eternal honeymoon with Jesus, the Bridegroom, the One referred to in some of our worship services as, "Sweetest Jesus."

God is doing a great work in us. He is forming Christ in us. Are we letting Him? Do we endeavor to come to know Him more personally? To grow in our love for Him? Are we yielding our will to His? Are we repenting? Are we following Him? Is our faith becoming more personal, and thus more real? Are we reflecting the personal love of God to those about us? Is our love for people becoming more personal?

I conclude with a magnificently personal Christmas prayer to Jesus by Metropolitan Philip of the Antiochian Archdiocese,

THE FEAST OF THE NATIVITY OF JESUS CHRIST

LORD,

What shall I offer you on your birthday in return for your infinite love?

I have neither gold nor silver, neither myrrh nor frankincense.

My house is without a roof. I have not room for you; not even a manger. My soul is even darker than the clouds of my passion. My eyes are too dim to look beyond the horizon of myself. Help me behold your bright star: "For in thy light we shall see light."

LORD,

You have been knocking on my door for thirty-nine years, but I never dared let you in because my garment is not white as snow.

Forgive me if I do not invite you to my table, for my table is full of everything you despise. I have denied you more than Peter.

I have doubted you more than Thomas.

I have betrayed you more than Judas.

My hands are empty. My lips are not clean to sing your praise.

And my heart is wrinkled with sorrow like a withered leaf under autumn's wind.

LORD,

The only thing I can offer you on your birthday is myself.

Drown me in the ocean of your love.

Feed me with your heavenly bread, for the bread of this world will never satisfy my hunger.

Quench my thirst with your divine fountain. For the water of this earth will never satisfy my thirst.

Give me your eyes to see what you see, your ears to hear what you hear and your heart to love what you love.

Take me with you to Mount Tabor and let me bathe in your eternal light.

LORD,

"Create a clean heart in me. Cast me not away from Thy face. Restore unto me the joy of Thy salvation, and strengthen me with a perfect spirit."

Teach me how to pray in simple words, for only through prayer I may overcome my loneliness.

Help me to care for the needy, the oppressed, the orphans, the sinners and the despised whom you love.

As I kneel before your manger with love and humility I beseech you to listen to my prayers.

"The Feast of the Nativity of Jesus Christ"
Appeared in the December 1994 issue of
"The Word." By Metropolitan Philip.